ALL-IN CAREGIVING

A GUIDE FOR THE CARE OF AGING PARENTS

Christine Klotz

Alfadore Press
Madison, Wisconson

All-In Caregiving: A Guide for the Care of Aging Parents

Copyright © 2018 Christine Klotz. All rights reserved.

Published by Alfadore Press, 7613 Elmwood Ave. #620416

Madison, WI 53562-0416

This book or parts thereof may not be reproduced in any form or method, stored in a retrieval system, or transmitted in any form by any means—electronic, mechanical, photocopy, recording, or otherwise—except as permitted under Section 107 or 108 of the 1976 United States Copyright Act, without either the prior written permission of the publisher, or authorization through payment of the appropriate per-copy fee. For more information go to www.alfadore.com.

Limit of Liability/Disclaimer of Warranty: While both the author and publisher used their best efforts in the writing and preparation of this book they make no representations or warranties with respect to the accuracy or completeness of its contents and they specifically disclaim any implied warranties for any particular purpose. The advice and strategies contained herein may not be suitable for your situation. You should consult with a professional where appropriate. Neither the publisher nor author shall be liable for any loss or any other damages, including but not limited to special, incidental, consequential, or other damages.

The information in this book is not intended to substitute for medical or legal advice. It is intended only to help individuals navigate the complex and sometimes dysfunctional health care system. Should you or anyone you help require legal or medical care you are advised to consult professionals who can provide the care.

    ISBN 978-1-947354-06-7 (trade paperback)
    ISBN 978-1-947354-07-4 (eBook)

ALFADORE
PRESS

More about the author:
www.alfadore.com

Acknowledgements

This book was inspired by many people I have known throughout my professional career including older adults, their families and the dedicated people who worked with them in healthcare settings and community.

I want to express special thanks to Carol Wehrley who at 95 years of age has been a great cheerleader. She tirelessly read and commented on every stage of the book's production from early drafts to the final copy.

Special thanks are also owed to beta readers Ann Albert, Betty Falco, Lisa Holmes, Jan Keen, and Daniel Klotz who helped strengthen the book and clean up rough edges. And a heartfelt thanks to my husband who pushed me and celebrated with me as the book took shape.

Any remaining errors or problems in the book are solely my own.

Contents

1	The four secrets of all-in caregiving	1
2	Relax! You're not your parent's parent	15
3	Enlist family help	41
4	What's coming and what you can do about it	53
5	When staying at home beats moving	69
6	Make medical decisions easier	83
7	Your best friends - *authority* and *guidelines*	97
8	Medical treatments you should know about	109
9	Advance Directives – your instruments of power	121
10	Your best choices in your parents final stages of life	137
11	Know this and be in control	151
12	How to be assertive at a doctor's appointment	169
13	Hospitalization happens!	185
14	Ten common hazards of hospitalization and what to do about them	197
15	Post-hospitalization complications and how to avoid them	229
16	The three pillars of all-in caregiving	241
Appendices		
Appendix A	7-point medication list	263

Appendix B Advance care planning in 4 easy steps	267
Index	277

1
The four secrets of all-in caregiving

So! Someone has told you that you are a family caregiver and you wonder what in the world that means. You probably feel a certain amount of resentment, confusion and uncertainty. Most people do when they find themselves in this position. You are not alone; most of us become caregivers at some time in our lives. I've been there, and probably will be again.

Being a caregiver can be all-consuming; exhausting. But it can also be fulfilling and rewarding, bringing you closer to a loved one who needs care.

Some people step willingly into the role of caregiver. They are emotionally and psychologically prepared to sacrifice to help loved ones who can no longer cope on their own. Others enter caregiving more grudgingly. Some have to be dragged into it kicking and screaming. Healthcare professionals too often assume family members are ready, willing, and able to take on the role and responsibilities of care for a loved one. You may think that it isn't fair that you have to take on this burden when you are already busy trying to meet all the demands of modern life.

At any rate, whether you were an inductee or volunteer, you are now faced with demands and requirements for which you were unprepared. But despite your doubts, you will discover that you can do this. You can prepare yourself for the challenges you will face as your parents age and need increasingly more support from you. You can develop the skills and knowledge to be a competent and confident caregiver. To be an *all-in* caregiver.

The goal of this book is to get you more prepared. To help you be a good caregiver without destroying your own life in the process. And, I might add, without seriously interfering with the lives of the rest of your family. Later in this chapter I will let you in on the four secrets of all-in caregiving. They are essential for you to know because they can make the difference between failed and successful caregiving. Between misery – for you and everyone involved – and a positive outcome of this period in your life. These four secrets are the crux of all-in caregiving and will be the focus of everything presented here.

Most people have no idea what it takes to be a caregiver until they become one. It takes stamina, patience, insight, compassion, knowledge, and of course time to take care of someone who is old, ill, or incapacitated. None of these qualities come to us without effort, and time is something few of us have enough of.

Hardly anyone is prepared for it, yet every day more and more people become unpaid family caregivers. In the short time it has taken you to read these introductory sentences, in the United States alone over 35 people have become unpaid family caregivers. It is estimated that on any given day in the U.S. there are over 40 million such caregivers.

Chapter 1. The four secrets of all-in caregiving

My perspectives on the role of the family caregiver come from years of professional experience plus the eye-opening example of my parents who in their 80s began a gradual decline accompanied by ever increasing needs.

After a lifetime of work in eldercare I had always assumed it would be my job to guide my family through the challenges that would arise as our parents grew older. The healthcare system in the United States is loaded with obstacles and challenges. For one thing older people who enter care delivery can be swept along with all the bells and whistles medical care has to offer. The focus on doing what is medically possible to keep someone alive at any cost ignores the softer (but perhaps more important) concepts of quality of life and what an older patient might actually want. Or not want, in the case of some types of treatment. Almost all patients, and especially older adults, need someone who can represent their interests and wishes.

There are also the obstacles and gaps in care that too often lead to poor health outcomes. These also call for someone to watch over an elder's best interests and care options.

When my parents reached their mid-80s they lived in their own home in California. My brother Peter and his wife Liz lived nearby and my other brother Dan lived within easy driving distance. I lived in New York. Having recently left a position as CEO of a healthcare organization in New York City, I was a consultant to a health foundation designing programs to help slow down the decline and frailty that older adults inevitably experience. Thus I had a wealth of experience to help my brothers, Liz, and me coordinate the support our parents needed.

Things proceeded relatively smoothly and we felt like we had things well under control. That is, until Mom experienced her first health crisis.

That event coincided with one of my frequent trips to California. After I got there I learned that Mom was experiencing pain in her groin. Peter had made a doctor's appointment for her and hoped I could take her. Not a problem, I thought.

The appointment was scheduled for mid-morning. Early on the day of the appointment I reminded Mom about her appointment so she would have plenty of time to get ready to go. I was on top of this and had everything under control.

Or so I thought. Mother had decided to be difficult that day. It turned out to be a real battle – a verbal and emotional tug-of-war – just to get her out the door and to her appointment.

There is a communication style that helps adults be in charge of their own health. Called coaching, I knew the subject well. But that day what I knew flew out the window and I blew it. My patience wore thin and instead of staying cool and searching for the right words to use, I got bossy. I began giving Mother directions and telling her what to do. Big mistake!

Mom was not a confrontational kind of person so she did not overtly reject my attempts at control. She used instead one of her more developed talents, dawdling. If there were an Olympic medal for dawdling she could have won the gold that day. On top of her natural disposition toward slowness, she did not want to go to the doctor. Her resistance that morning was mostly passive. You know, being quietly obstinate and uncooperative, resisting in ways sometimes hard to define.

It became obvious to me later that she did not want the doctor to know about her groin pain because she was afraid of what he might say. She was afraid she might have to go to the hospital. Or worse.

Most older adults clearly want to stay in their own homes for the rest of their lives. A fear that underlies many actions and responses as people age is the fear that they will be required to move to a nursing home. This fear is reinforced by horror stories of abandonment and mistreatment that make it seem like all nursing homes are dungeons of horror. Added to that is the pervasive belief that healthcare authorities are looking for reasons to tell older adults that they can no longer live at home.

In truth, nursing homes have worked hard to improve life for the people who live in them. But they are not the only alternative for senior living. In fact only four percent of older adults live in nursing homes. Improvements in home-based care options have meant that not every older person will face time at the end of their lives in some kind of care facility. Nonetheless, the fear of having to leave home and "get put away" is very real for many seniors. They dread the loss of control, perhaps even the loss of all purpose in living, thinking of nursing home existence as being put on a shelf just waiting to die.

Mom's groin pain had been the result of a fall and she was well aware that falls are one of the most common reasons older adults have to leave their homes. That was what Mom was worried about, afraid her fall had put her at risk of being unable to remain in her own home. She had convinced herself that if she just took it easy for a few days the pain would go away.

But she was in a lot of pain so waiting was not an option. She could only walk a few steps at a time because of the pain, so she had to be moved using Dad's wheelchair. Which of course triggered even more resistance from Mom. Finally, with Liz's help, we got both Mom and the wheelchair into the car and Mom and I headed off for her appointment.

When we arrived at her doctor's office and presented ourselves at the receptionist's station it dawned on me that I had not come prepared. We did not have Mom's Medicare card. In fact, we had not even brought her wallet, so we had no ID for her, nothing. Fortunately the receptionist was understanding and said that if nothing had changed they had all the information they needed on file.

It turned out that Mom's regular doctor was out of the office that day and another doctor was covering for him. This introduced a whole new opportunity for Mom to hone her passive aggressive skills. First of all, she did not want to see a new doctor, one who was unknown to her. Plus she was sure her doctor really was there and just didn't want to see her. This irrational notion was undoubtedly due to some cognitive impairment Mom had begun to have, and no amount of reasoning from me was going to dispel her paranoid thoughts about the missing doctor's whereabouts.

To say that the examination didn't go well is an understatement. First of all, Mom refused to answer questions put to her by the doctor. He asked her how she had fallen. Silence. He asked where she hurt. Silence. She would just ignore his questions and look off into the distance. At one point, when the physician stepped out for a moment, Mom said she did not know this doctor and she was not going to tell him anything about herself.

I renewed my attempt to reason with her but again to no avail.

When the doctor returned he directed all of his questions to me instead of Mom. When he asked me what medications she was taking I realized yet another mistake I had made. I had not brought Mom's list of medications. Forehead slap! It was posted in plain view in the kitchen and I should have brought it along. I could only remember a few of the drugs she took.

Mom knew all of her medications and could have answered the question, but the doctor had stopped addressing any questions or comments to her, and Mom was proving good to her word. Her lips were sealed.

The doctor asked me what I knew about the origin of her pain, what had happened, and when the pain started. Blank, blank, and blank. I didn't know the answers to any of the questions. All I had been told by Peter was that she had probably fallen a couple of days earlier. The doctor was visibly displeased by my lack of specifics and asked me yet more questions. I told him I was from out of state and had just arrived the evening before. It had been my brother who had arranged the medical appointment.

The doctor made no attempt to mask his exasperation and asked why my brother hadn't brought her in since I was not able to be of much help. His absence of courtesy and tact stunned me. I was speechless.

In principle he was of course right. I should have been prepared to give the details of Mom's situation and to speak on her behalf. Clearly I was not. I did not have the kind of information needed for her diagnosis or treatment management. I had mistakenly assumed she would speak for herself.

It was during this horrible doctor's appointment that I came to a very important realization. I had been so busy being the expert I had missed something far more important. Mom didn't need an expert, a seasoned healthcare executive with big city experience to give orders and tell everyone what to do. What she and Dad needed more than anything was emotional support and advocacy for their wishes.

The appropriate role for me was primordial, a role as ancient as humankind itself, a role I had had since long before I had anything called a career. That role was Daughter! That was Job One for me with my folks: To be their daughter. Their champion. Their advocate. And to give them emotional support.

I was clearly unprepared to be Mom's advocate at her doctor's appointment. I should have prepared myself by asking more questions of my brother and mother before she was in the clinical situation and overwhelmed by stress. Before fear got the better of her. Somehow we made it through the doctor's visit, then we were sent to another facility for x-rays. That's where we learned that Mom had a pelvic fracture.

While sitting in the x-ray center's waiting room a woman asked if we were mother and daughter. The look of pride that question brought to Mom's face affected me deeply. That experience galvanized my resolve to step up to bat and be the best advocate I could for my mother.

An opportunity to put that resolve into action occurred almost immediately. We were told to return to the doctor's office to find out the result of the x-rays and I said we were not going to do that. I told the technician in the x-ray office to call Mom's doctor's office for instructions, that we had no intention of driving all the way back across town just for that. My firmness paid off. The doctor relayed his instructions to us over the phone. Mom was to take it easy for a couple of weeks to allow her pelvis to heal. It was ironic that, after all the difficulties of the day, Mom had been right after all. She did not need any medical treatment.

At the time of this episode my family had already been working together to support Dad who had experienced a stroke a few years earlier. My parents declined in health over a period of about seven years. Starting with Dad's stroke and then a few years later both he and Mom started having illnesses and injuries that reduced their ability to manage on their own. My brothers, Liz, and I coordinated with our parents to provide the support they needed to meet their goal to remain in their home.

When I was around my folks, whether taking them to medical appointments, doing things around their home, or just visiting with them, I was their daughter. I was not a healthcare big shot in their house. My decades of experience in healthcare were not likely to be of much help if I was not paying attention to their emotional state at the moment, and what they might be thinking. It was of paramount importance for me to know how they were feeling in the then-and-there.

It took awhile for me to become a good listener to my parents. I needed to listen more, and I needed to listen better. We all know there is listening, and then there is *listening*. It is easy to convince ourselves that we are listening because we are paying attention, hearing and understanding the words. But often we do that without really hearing the meaning of what is being said. Perhaps more importantly, what is being said *between* the words.

Effective listening can prove difficult for family members. The communication in families is affected, often distorted, by layers of complication from shared experiences and the emotional overtones from the family roles we each play.

Every time I visited my folks I could see numerous ways to help, changes that would make their lives safer and easier. Unfortunately they almost always rejected my suggestions out of hand. So I learned to keep my observations to myself and give them to my brothers. They could then gradually bring up my suggestions at opportune times. That worked a lot better. Gradual and repeated suggestions for change can go a long way toward overcoming the resistance to change that is a natural human characteristic. A characteristic that becomes stronger with age.

In the beginning I had been guilty of being the typical long-distance caregiver, flying in from out of town, ready to dive in and fix things.

Like most caregivers, I just wanted to help. But as with most older adults, there was a delicate balance in the circumstances of my parents' lives, a stasis that made it possible for them to continue to live together, in their home of many years, more or less autonomously. Anyone or anything that showed up on their doorstep with ideas for change was a potential threat to their stasis and would meet with resistance. As I have already said, there are ways to deal with this, but they must accommodate the elders' *need to control their lives.*

Most people take it as a given that everyone deserves to have as much control over their lives as possible. Helping elderly parents stay in charge of as much of their lives as possible is important. This requires more of that quality kind of listening I just referred to, in addition to a sensitivity to elders' evolving needs. In many cases it also calls for less *doing-for* and more *helping-with*.

When parents start to need help it is not the adult child's responsibility to take over all decision making and become a parent to the parent. Yet, too often, this is exactly what happens.

Being an advocate and champion for your parents requires knowledge and information. Being well informed is essential. This comes back to listening. You must prompt your parents to give you information, and you must listen carefully to what they say.

It is important to understand your parents' wishes for the last years of their lives and to keep *their* goals, not your own, as your guide. This is the only way to successfully support them. Guessing what you think they would want is not a good way to advocate for your parents. Know their wishes ahead of time so you can make informed decisions on their behalf when they are no longer able to make their own decisions.

Being a good advocate also means being able to say no. Problems can be caused by well-meaning professionals who are trained to solve health issues by treating whatever conditions and symptoms they see in their patients. Too often children are talked into accepting treatments their parents would have rejected.

Two common examples of this are *tests* and *surgical interventions*. Most older adults would opt to reject an uncomfortable test with meaningless results. That is, a test that provides information not likely to be acted upon. Many would also reject a high-risk surgery that could result in the rest of their life being spent in an intensive care unit.

This book will help you learn about the types of choices caregivers are commonly required to make. You can then talk with your parents to learn their wishes. That way when an untoward health event comes along and you have to step up to make a decision you will know how to evaluate the care options based on their wishes and goals. Later I'll tell you how to structure this kind of conversation and have the best chance of getting the right information about the right topics.

Knowing your parents' wishes ahead of time will help you deal with the fear that can drive one to make bad choices. The fear of losing a parent, or of making a wrong decision (because we don't know their wishes ahead of time) can lead to bad decisions. Prepare ahead of time to avoid fear-driven bad decisions.

None of this need be confusing. Difficult at times because of the importance of the issues, but not confusing. From years of experience working with people in situations just like yours I can assure you there is a way to end your confusion, learn what you need to know, and be an effective and successful caregiver. As I mentioned earlier, there are four categories essential to being a confident and capable caregiver. These four areas will be spelled out for you in this book:

1. *Personal preparation.* Prepare yourself to be the kind of caregiver you really want to be. It is not that difficult once you know how to do it.

2. *Health partnership.* Help your parent be a stronger partner with medical professionals and participate in care decisions.

3. *Health advocate.* Protect your loved one from many of the potential hazards of hospital and medical care.

4. *Parental representative.* Be confident that you know and can follow the paths that your parents or other loved one would choose for themselves if they were able to make the decisions themselves.

Because most family caregivers provide care to a parent, most frequently a mother, I will often refer to a "parent" for simplicity. The same principles will apply regardless of whether it is your spouse, another relative, or anyone else you love who is aging and dealing with loss of function.

In the next chapter we delve into your role as a family caregiver. That will be followed by information that will help you understand personal care choices that support aging in place.

By the way, in case you are not familiar with the phrase "aging in place," it simply means staying at home as long as possible. The *place* is wherever your folks have been living. If they can stay there, without having to move into some kind of care center, they will be aging in place. This is a desirable goal for almost all aging people.

Some of the more difficult choices and decisions caregivers will make focus on end-of-life decisions. But most caregivers need to step in to support and advocate for parents' choices and values years before making end-of-life decisions. Several chapters will explore choices for living and choices for care. These will be followed by guidance regarding the preparation of advance directive documents.

If an older person lives long enough it is likely that he or she will experience at least some loss in cognitive function that impacts the ability to think, reason, and make decisions. For some this will be dementia that eventually causes more serious incapacity. Before that can happen you want to know your parents' wishes and move forward with the legal preparations allowed in the state where your parents live. These steps allow someone to act and make decisions for another person when she is no longer able to speak for herself.

Several chapters will give you guidance about care choices for older adults. This will enable you to be an *empowered* caregiver. Being prepared will not only help you advocate for your parents' wishes but will also prepare you to avoid possible hazards and risks resulting from care in a doctor's office or in a hospital.

In chapter 16 you will find practical advice on how to put the pillars of all-in caregiving in place to help you and your parents manage their care over the final years of their lives. You will also read some suggestions for taking care of yourself; you will find it difficult to be of help to your parents if you don't take care of yourself.

The appendix provides two items you are likely to find quite helpful:

- *Medication List* template.

- *Advance Care Planning in 4 Easy Steps.*

Set your overall objective to become an informed and empowered caregiver, as well as an active care partner and champion when your loved one encounters the healthcare system. The next chapter will focus on the changing roles that result from the responsibility of caregiving and begin your preparation toward becoming an exceptional caregiver.

2
Relax! You're not your parent's parent

SOONER OR LATER everyone needs help, and someone has to provide it. An aging or disabled family member or friend is likely to be the one who needs help, and it is a spouse or an adult child who becomes the helper. As you become a helper remember this is a *new* role; you are not assuming the role of parent to the person you help.

It is likely, since you are reading this, that the role of caregiver has somehow landed on your shoulders. You might be feeling overwhelmed by the enormity of it all and wondering how on earth you will cope with your new responsibilities.

It probably did not start out being this overwhelming. It just crept up on you as your occasional help became more and more frequent whether you were prepared for it or not. Before you knew it you were an unpaid family caregiver.

Sometimes the caregiver role is temporary because of, say, an injury or acute illness. Advanced age and frailty, though, is most often the major reason care is needed for a longer period of time. Because the debilitating insults and injuries of advancing age are seldom completely reversed, the role of temporary caregiver in many cases becomes permanent.

It surprises many that the metamorphosis to family caregiver does not change the fundamental relationship between the caregiver and the one he or she cares for. The original role – spouse, child, friend – is never lost. This is especially true in the case of parent-child situations. As pointed out in the previous chapter, no matter how dependent parents might become on their adult child's care, the parent-child relationship will forever remain primary. Once a child – in the sense of offspring – always a child.

This may be why there is so much resistance to being labeled a *family caregiver*. Most family members are uncomfortable with that label which is so often given to them by healthcare professionals. After all, the caregiver's thinking seems to be, they are just doing what any caring spouse or child would do when their loved one needs a bit of extra help. Slapping a formal label like that on what they do feels like it demeans their efforts and their caring concern. Calling them a caregiver might feel like a demotion from caring daughter, son, spouse, or friend.

Perceived as a demotion or not, it is happening to a constantly rising percentage of the American population. More and more people are finding themselves caregivers or receivers. We hear daily about the aging of the U.S. population. Baby boomers are entering the ranks of the over 65 group in record numbers. People are living longer and generally are in better health for a longer period of time. In fact, in the over-65 age group, the number of those over 85 is growing very fast. More people are living to 90 and 100 than ever before.

An aging population like ours means there are more people who experience a stage of decline that lasts for many years. And it is those who care about them who most likely end up caring for them.

Add to this the fact that hospital stays are shorter than they used to be. Shorter hospital stays mean families must do many of the things that in years past were done by doctors and nurses. Abbreviated institutional care means extended home care.

Geography is another factor. Nuclear families are no longer concentrated in one place like they once were. Family members are often spread across the country. As a result, children and other extended family members live far away from the aging relative who needs help. This adds additional layers of stress, expense and difficulty to the role of being a caregiver.

The concept of family is also changing. There are many more adults who are single and live alone through choice, divorce, and other reasons. And remarriage can make it possible for a son or daughter to have more than four older adults who can potentially need help. Add aunts, uncles and other extended family members and the likelihood of being called upon to be a caregiver greatly increases.

You may be willing to step in to help with care needs but fitting these new responsibilities into your daily routine can be difficult. In 2016 the Population Reference Bureau reported that almost half of the U.S. population over the age of 65 needs help with routine daily living activities from shopping to meal preparation to bathing. Most of their care comes from family members. In fact, more than 95 percent of care provided to older adults who do not live in senior living facilities is provided by family members.

Providing this kind of care can be a positive experience that increases feelings of closeness, plus it is nice to know that a loved one is being cared for with compassion and in the best way possible.

On the other hand, for many this role is stressful and financially challenging. This is especially true when a family caregiver has to struggle to balance work and other family responsibilities. And there is often the issue of whether or not the caregiver has the physical ability to handle the required tasks.

More than half of family caregivers have jobs and work outside the home. Their caregiving demands can lead to loss of income from missed work or the need to work reduced hours. While many sons and husbands provide care to family members, the vast majority of caregivers are women.

Meanwhile the role of daughter or son continues and will never change even as the role of family caregiver has been added. What being a *caregiver* means, exactly, is not always clear. In a study conducted jointly by the National Alliance for Caregiving and AARP, it was found that there is no simple definition for the role of family caregivers. They share many common struggles, but they have many different needs for support.[1]

An in-depth look at this important role estimated that 34 million people in the United States provide unpaid care each year to an adult over 50 years of age. Some estimates range as high as 30 billion hours that are devoted every year to taking care of elderly family members and friends. The vast majority care for a relative. About half care for a parent, but it is spouses who provide the most hours of care.

Here is something that might sound familiar to you: About half of the caregivers said that they did not have a choice in whether or not to take on the role of caregiver. And that role they were locked into will continue, on average, for more than four years.

If you add up the hours you spend each week as a caregiver, you will likely find you approach the average in the study. That is, about 24 hours a week.

It is also likely you feel that you are not getting adequate information to help you provide the care that is needed. Studies have shown that 66 percent of caregivers say no one has even bothered to ask them what kind of help and support they need to care for their family member.

That bears repeating for emphasis: Two-thirds of the people who are providing care to family members have never been asked what they need to provide this care. When asked, caregivers say they need more information, especially on how to keep their loved one safe. That is followed closely by a need for information on how to better manage their own stress. Again, this probably sounds familiar to you.

Caregiving responsibilities can build gradually, or they can occur suddenly when a person is thrust into the role of caregiver quickly. This often occurs following a crisis for a loved one. Like your mother has fallen and broken her hip, your father has just had a stroke, or your wife collapsed while having lunch with a friend. The unpleasant possibilities are almost limitless.

Once something like this happens, your life as you knew it is changed in the blink of an eye. For most people the only certainty is that you want to help, to do whatever needs to be done to help your loved one and get everything back to normal. You have been thrust into a new normal that is still being defined. The old normal doesn't exist anymore. Not only that, the new normal is just temporary and will last only as long as nothing else happens. It might be years before something else happens, or it could be tomorrow.

This is one of the most stressful aspects of being a caring family member. Everything becomes uncertain. Now you are afraid to ever be out of range of the phone. You avoid situations and circumstances that might render you unable to help when needed. It is hard to plan anything because you realize you have very little influence on what the future holds. Plans and projects get put on hold. Such as family vacations. What would you do if something happened to Dad while you were away? Could you get back in time to help?

If you don't live nearby, even a couple of hours distance can make everything more of a challenge. Any time you phone Mom and don't get an answer, the worst scenarios take hold of your imagination. What's wrong? Is Mom just in the garden or out with friends, or has she fallen and can't get to the phone? Should you drop everything to go find out? Or are you over-reacting?

Even simple things like ordinary doctor's appointments become problematic if you have to include an hour or two of travel time to get there. Your personal and family needs get put on the back burner and it can go on this way for years.

Many well-meaning people refer to this change to becoming a parent's caregiver as a *role reversal*. A son or daughter might delude themselves into believing they have become the parent. But in my work with many older people and their adult children (and in my personal experience, too) I can unequivocally say that this is not the case. No matter what happens to your parents' health, you are always a son or daughter first in their eyes. To them you can never be the parent. Be your folks' advocate. Be their champion. But never try to assume the role of their parent.

Those of us who find ourselves in the role of caregiver have to find ways to support our historical relationships as we take on tasks that can be quite personal and intimate. Sometimes this just means finding ways to allow your dad to stay in control of anything that it is still possible for him to do. It helps if you make it clear that you are doing things *with* him to help him, not to take charge and do things *to* him. This might be as simple as just asking permission for some tasks.

Once I had a primary care physician who asked permission for everything when he examined me. He would ask, "Is it okay if I listen to your heart now?" "May I look in your ears?" At first I thought this was odd. After all, I was the patient and he was the physician. He was the one who was supposed to be the authority. It finally dawned on me that his asking permission for everything was his way of showing respect for me as a person, allowing me to feel at least some control. This is an important lesson for all of us when we take on the care of older family members.

After Dad had had a stroke I went with him to some of his rehabilitation therapy sessions. I wanted to observe his therapy so I would know how to help him when he was at home.

During one of his last therapy sessions Dad was scheduled to work with an occupational therapist to learn how to get into a bathtub. Dad mentioned to the therapist that I had been an occupational therapist and she was pleased to be able to share my dad's abilities and needs with someone who understood what she was doing.

There was a shower in the therapy center and the therapist wanted to make this a real experience. That is, Dad was going to actually take a shower with guidance from the therapist. She told me the plan and said, "Come on in."

I hesitated. I had never seen my dad naked. Over the years of working in healthcare I was accustomed to seeing men in various states of undress, but this was my dad! On the other hand I did need to see what he was able to do so I would know how much help Mom would need to support him at home.

I resolved this quandary by asking Dad if he minded me being in the room. He said he didn't mind at all. That was much better for both of us than it would have been had I just walked in. By asking I re-framed the situation. As a result neither of us was embarrassed. It only took a second for me to ask and it was the right thing to do.

Over time, as the care you provide becomes more involved, routinely asking permission for every action can become cumbersome and downright annoying to everyone. That does not mean, however, that you should not try, in any way possible, to help the person you love hang onto their dignity and sense of who they are. Maybe you just ask if she is ready or you can find some other way to help your parent feel in control instead of feeling like things are just being done to her.

One of the greatest fears of aging is the fear of losing one's sense of self. This is a very real concern for almost all elderly people, whether they could articulate it or not. Progressive frailty and (often) cognitive decline, two of the more common features of getting old, make it difficult for an elder to maintain her ego and sense of self. Caregivers, who respond by treating elders like children, make the relationship stressful and much more difficult. Treat them in the same way one would treat a child and the result is typically an increase in the stress between the older person and the one providing care.

As some have said, ageism begins at home when family members remove responsibility for both the big and little decisions in daily life.

Stripping elders of their independence usually starts small, say when a family member takes charge of paying bills. This can easily escalate to an appropriation of all decision making, leaving nothing for the care recipient to decide. If caregivers make all the decisions – when baths will take place, what foods will be eaten and when, what clothes will be worn, and so on – nothing is left to bolster the identity of the person being cared for. Eventually most interactions devolve into task-oriented procedures with little human warmth and only functional touching. The focus comes to be on tasks that have to get done. Warmth, respect and affection get left behind. It is too easy in the midst of all the demands and requirements of caregiving to forget that as a spouse, daughter, or son, we also need to respect and support the individuality and personhood of the family member in need of care.

A frail older person's transition to the need for help with their personal care is a significant time for both the elder and the family. Families cope with this in different ways. One couple I knew, who had been married for 60 years, arrived at a time in their lives when the husband needed help dressing and bathing. His wife decided it was time to get help. In her words, she was a wife, not a nurse, and she was quite adamant that she was not going to be turned into one.

In contrast are those couples in which one spouse gradually assumes the personal care tasks of the other, and he or she would be offended by any suggestion that home care staff be brought in to help.

Every person, every couple, every family is different. Some family members can comfortably take on very intimate tasks while others cannot. One daughter told me her favorite time was helping her mother with her bath. It was a calm time away from other distractions when they could chat and reminisce about family experiences.

Many people find it difficult to accept help with bathing, but sometimes the only safe way it can be done is with help. And being helped, even though uncomfortable, is better than having to settle for an inadequate sponge bath at a sink.

For some people the help of a stranger is easier to accept than help from a family member. In situations like this, hiring a home care aide to come in once or twice a week to help with bathing may be the answer. Whether from family or an aide, some older adults are thrilled to have help because they can finally bathe again safely without fear. Sometimes frail elders have had nothing but sponge baths for months because they are afraid to get into the shower or bathtub. For them indignity and loss of privacy takes a back seat to the luxury of being clean.

When your care recipient goes to the hospital or rehabilitation center the staff will ask her about her ability to complete everyday tasks. In fact, it is likely that several different staff members will ask about them. They will want to know which things she is able to handle herself, and for which ones she needs help.

Healthcare professionals break down the routine activities of daily living into six general categories:

- *Eating.* Can she feed herself? Does she have trouble swallowing?

- *Bathing.* Can she get in and out of a shower or bathtub by herself? Does she have difficulty washing her hair? Can she lather and rinse herself adequately?

- *Personal hygiene and grooming.* Can she brush her teeth and comb her hair herself?

- *Dressing.* What kinds of problems, if any, does she have getting dressed?

- *Toileting.* Can she go to the bathroom independently or does she need assistance?

- *Functional mobility.* Can she get in and out of bed on her own? Can she move from one place to another on her own? Does she use any equipment like a walker or cane?

When asked, be prepared to give detailed information about how well your loved one can perform these activities of daily living.

There are also the *instrumental* activities of daily living. These are less personal but still necessary to live independently at home. Some of the more common instrumental tasks are:

- *Meal preparation.* Can she cook and fix meals on her own?

- *Housekeeping.* How capable is she with cleaning and maintaining her home?

- *Medication management.* Does she know which prescribed medications she takes and when to take them? Does she reliably remember to take them at the right time?

- *Transportation management.* Does she still drive? Can she adequately make use of public transportation?

- *Money management.* Can she reliably manage a checkbook? Pay bills?

- *Shopping.* Is she able to shop for groceries and other necessities?

As you can see, the instrumental activities of daily living are things that can be taken care of by someone else. While necessary for community living, they do not need to be completed by the older person. In fact it is possible that your care recipient never developed skills for some of these tasks. For example some older women never managed household financial matters and some men never cleaned the house. And anyone who lives where there is good public transportation may never have needed to learn to drive an automobile.

Most people will lose their ability to complete the instrumental activities of daily living (the second list above) long before they need help with the routine, or more personal, activities of daily living (the first list). Family and friends frequently find the instrumental tasks to be the easiest ones to step in and help with. Most instrumental tasks can be taken care of by purchasing services if one has the financial resources.

Some examples of ways to bring in help for instrumental activities of daily living include having home-delivered meals, hiring a cleaning service, or using transportation services in the community. If you need help finding out what community services might be available to provide meals, transportation or other support, a good resource is your local office for aging[2] or your community senior center.

When family members are available to step in to help, this typically starts with one or two instrumental activities of living. Picking up medications, filling a pill box, providing a ride to medical appointments or the grocery store, and at some point becoming power of attorney to handle bills and financial matters. Most of these tasks can be done on a flexible schedule at convenient times. But keep in mind that even these tasks may be viewed by a parent or other older care recipient as an infringement of their autonomy and control. Many elders put up a lot of resistance to help with their instrumental activities.

Find ways to include your parent in these tasks. Take bill paying as an example. An elder will retain more of his sense of control if you review with him which bills are to be paid. You can also leave the signing of the checks to him after you have them ready.

With a little ingenuity you can come up with ways to keep your older parent involved in the routines of living. They must be non-trivial ways, but they need not be the major aspects of the activity. There just needs to be enough involvement for the elder to retain a sense of at least some control. This will not only make life easier for everyone involved, it is more compassionate.

The areas of personal care are more challenging. What happens when your mother calls and says she wants you to come to her house because she can't put on her shoes? When a person is no longer able to perform the personal activities of daily living, help and support become urgent and more frequent. If your mom can't put on her shoes she will not want to sit idly for hours waiting for you to get away from other responsibilities to come help her. Your worry is that she won't wait, that she will get hurt trying to put them on herself.

Some aspects of personal care require more skill than others. Like getting out of bed, for example. There are right and wrong ways to help someone safely get out of bed and dressed. There can be serious risks if it is done incorrectly, both for the helper and the helpee. These are the kinds of things you should ask about. Most healthcare professionals are happy to give instructions on how to safely help your aging loved ones with personal care. Professionals can also tell you how you can help your loved one become more independent. This may include use of various assistive devices to make it easier to dress, bathe and complete other daily living tasks.

No matter how prepared and careful you are, an accident or illness can strike at any time. When an accident does happen, or your loved one gets sick and must be taken in for treatment, be prepared to answer a lot of questions.

Let's use that earlier example from my own experience and say that your mother has suffered a fall. When you take her for treatment the therapists and clinical staff will want details on what she was able to do on her own before her accident. This will help them assess what she will need to work on as she moves forward in recovery.

In clinical situations it is not unusual for older adults to claim they can manage everything by themselves. They will say they can handle all the activities of daily living on their own. And they might very well believe that at the moment they are saying it. They quite naturally believe they can do everything they have always been able to do.

It is safe to say that most humans do not gracefully accept the onset of wrinkles and gray hair. It is even harder to accept the loss of basic abilities. Someone who all his life has been able to put on his socks and shoes, fry an egg for breakfast, or quickly clamber in and out of a bathtub may find it incomprehensible that such independence is coming to an end. When common everyday activities get difficult, the mind rebels. So it should not be surprising when an elder believes he can do more than he actually can.

It takes close, personal observation to keep up with your parents' capabilities. Remember, you will need to know what your dad was able to do before his illness, or what your mother could do before her accident. The more accurately you can report such things, the better will therapists know what goals are realistic for what they call "returned function" following a period of therapy.

Also remember that professionals sometimes presume too much. It is not uncommon for them to reckon that any close family member within sight can completely disrupt her life to take care of someone. If you don't step up to do whatever is needed, you can be made to feel inadequate by healthcare professionals who shamelessly make assumptions for you that they would never make for themselves.

Like the case of a man whose mother needed help managing her medications. The man, who runs his own business, was told by a physician, "Make sure your mother takes her medications three times a day." How do you suppose the physician would have responded to being told the same thing? "Leave your practice three times a day to go to your mother's house and see that she takes her medications."

The man had to arrange for a home health aide to be with his mother during the day to help her. And to make sure she took her medications. This arrangement had gone on for just a short time when he was told by a home health nurse that his mother needed too much care to be able to safely remain in the home.

Now, this man's mother was mentally capable of making her own decisions and she didn't want to leave her home. But her son, unsure what to do, thought he had to accept the home health nurse's opinion. The son was worried that he would get into trouble if he did not follow the nurse's recommendation and move his mother to an assisted living facility. Fortunately, after thinking about it and seeking advice, he decided to ignore the nurse's recommendation. He did not *have* to do anything and his mother stayed at home, where she wanted to be.

There will probably be plenty of times when you are in doubt. It is not unusual to be overwhelmed and feel inadequate with all the tasks of caregiving. As mentioned previously, some studies of families providing care for older adults have found that fewer than one in three caregivers feel prepared to provide the required care. I suspect that even those few who do think they are up to the task at the time of questioning are unaware of how their confidence will wither in the face of what's in store for them. Their responses might not be fully informed because it is hard to know what you don't know before a new situation happens.

It is an unfortunate fact that surprises are more the rule than the exception in caregiving. It is impossible to accurately predict how loved ones' needs will change.

Caregivers might feel prepared to provide the level of care and service needed in the current circumstances, but not prepared for what happens in subsequent months. The goal of every caregiver should be to constantly strive to be more and better prepared.

You are likely to be confronted with changes in your role with, and relationship to, the person who is the object of your caregiving. Both you and the one you are caring for will find life much easier if you resist the urge to completely take over.

Give thought to ways your mother can help and provide input into all your caregiving activities, especially in the kitchen if she is the one who has always done most of the cooking. Welcome her instructions on how to do something or on the selection of which utensils to use. Remember, it is her kitchen. Maybe she can help make salad or set the table. Whatever she is able to do, let her do it and you will be making dinner together instead of taking over and pushing her aside.

Be assured that once your mother begins to need help, you are in it for the long haul. Even if at some point it becomes necessary for her to move to another living setting, such as senior housing or assisted living or a nursing home, your job is not done until the end of her life.

It is hard and challenging work but when asked to talk about their experience most caregivers say they would do it all over again if they had to. They frequently report that caring for a spouse or parent brought them closer together and helped them come to a better understanding of one another. And of the family in general.

Because of my professional experience with seniors I am frequently asked for advice on how to help aging parents. This almost always starts with a request for ideas to help a parent stay safe at home. I also hear requests for help on how to decide when it is time to move parents out of their home and into an assisted living or nursing home. Safety is often the biggest concern expressed by the adult child. From listening to many older adults over the years, though, I can say that safety is generally not an older person's biggest concern.

Fear can be a strong motivator for both action and inaction. We want to help our aging parent but we don't know how. And we don't know where to get the information we need. Some don't want to admit to their fears or even that they need help. Fortunately there are services in every community that can help, and you can find information and resources through an internet search.

Many communities have information and referral services that you can contact to find what you need to support your parents. Again one of the best sources for local information is the office for aging or health department.

Adult children tend to rush in to help when parents need help. We are all busy with our own lives. Jumping in to solve the problem is faster than helping our parents handle problem situations themselves. Tying a shoe for an elder is much faster than waiting while they struggle to tie it themselves. We want to show concern and often do it by taking over and just doing what needs doing. We mistakenly think that fixing everything ourselves shows how much we care.

However, doing things for someone who is capable of doing them himself leads to dependence. This has also been shown to lead to cognitive decline. It is harmful to complete their sentences or answer questions for them without giving them a chance to do it themselves. Your dad's answer might be slow. He might not even know the answer. But answering for him does not save him from possible embarrassment. Reinforce who your dad is and allow him to contribute to conversations and activities. This will help him stay more independent and keep his mind sharper.

The best of intentions can sometimes go awry. Once I saw a chair in the middle of my mother's bedroom which was clearly what all the fall prevention guidelines call a *fall hazard*. I started to move it. Mom abruptly stopped me, letting me know that the chair served an important purpose which was to actually prevent a fall. She told me that when she got up in the middle of the night she was unsteady for the first few steps. By placing the chair in the middle of her usual pathway, a few steps from her bed, she had something she could use to steady herself before continuing to the bathroom.

The chair in the middle of the room was actually a good idea once Mom had explained it to me.

Most falls happen in the home so it is important to find ways to make it as safe as possible. Before you barge in and start making changes, however, ask yourself how you would like it if someone came into your home and started rearranging furniture, removing rugs, and installing grab bars in your bathroom. In my case we were in Mom's home and she hadn't asked me to help make it safer. While I was the daughter, I was also a guest. What worked for her might be in opposition to conventional fall-risk advice, but the chair was something that had served her well. You will recall that she did indeed experience a fall, but it did not happen in the bedroom .

Here is another example from my experience as a daughter. My parents ate Meals on Wheels on a typical day but the meals were only delivered Monday through Friday. When I was there visiting I would cook for them so I could stock their freezer with meals to supplement what they got from Meals on Wheels. I bought storage containers just for that purpose.

My parents seemed to appreciate the meals I prepared, but on my next visit I noticed that the storage containers were all missing. When I asked Mom about it she said she had thrown them away. She said they got along just fine with their Meals on Wheels.

I was initially offended by that, but after thinking about it I realized that this was an issue of threat to her as a parent and homemaker. Dad seemed to appreciate the meals but it was not his toes I was stepping on. It was Mom's. She was the one in control of their meals and she exercised that control by heating up the fare from Meals on Wheels and adding a salad she made herself.

Meals on Wheels was a more or less distant institution which was not a potential replacement for her. With the meals they delivered she could put a meal on the table without much work. With a few added touches of her own she felt she was still a wife and homemaker.

But when part of the meal came from me it challenged her roles as wife, homemaker, and mother. Hence her rebellion by discarding the containers I bought. Whether they ever actually ate the meals I put away for them, I'll never know.

Just as role threat can be a problem, so can loneliness, even in the presence of other family members. Consider this case of a woman who was in her 80s at the time. She had in-home care several days a week to help with housework, grocery shopping, errands, and bathing. In addition, her son would come to her home at least twice a week. He set up her pill box, checked on things around the house, took care of needed home maintenance, made sure the plants were watered and the grass mowed, and anything else that needed taking care of.

Yet this woman complained that she was lonely, that no one ever came to visit her. This despite the fact that people came to her house every day just to tend to her needs. The problem for her was that everyone concentrated on taking care of tasks. No one gave her any personal attention. No one took the time to sit down with her, even briefly, to chat a bit, share a personal story, discuss a bit of news or the weather.

Even more importantly, no one physically touched her except during routine tasks like helping her dress or bathe, or steadying her when she walked. Her sense of isolation and loneliness was real even though she was practically surrounded by people much of the time. What she needed was *personal* attention. She wanted someone to listen to her, to share a bit of themselves with her in an ordinary conversation.

She longed for a gentle touch, something more than what was required for tasks to be completed. She needed some nonverbal expression of concern, of caring. To know that someone else was really there for her and that she mattered to her son.

Her son was defensive about her complaints, which showed that he did not really hear her. He was doing his best to keep her safe in her home, juggling her needs while maintaining balance with his work and his own family. He was making many sacrifices to ensure her safety and comfort. Yet she complained.

The tension that arose between the son and his mother was unfortunate and would not have developed if he had just taken a few minutes while he was there to visit with her. *Really* visit with her, up close and personal, talk briefly about something that was important to her.

Lots of people have trouble with the talking part, with conversationally bridging the gap between generations. Adult children are frequently at a loss to know what to talk about with their elderly parents. When they do take the time to talk to them, all they hear is complaints about how rarely they talk. It becomes frustrating, so they stop trying.

One way to avoid this problem is to initiate discussions with parents about their lives before they had children. This gives them an enjoyable opportunity to talk about themselves. It is those earlier, more distant memories that are often the easiest ones for older people to remember. If you ask them about earlier times in their lives you are likely to learn things about them you never knew. You will probably hear stories you have never heard before. You will also be building up a storehouse of topics for later conversations.

It is wise to collect and preserve parents' stories because one day those memories will be gone forever. After your parents are gone it is too late to ask questions. Like, "What ever happened to so-and-so?" or, "What did you think when you first saw a cell phone?" With a little thought you can probably come up with a long list of questions like this.

Some people are good at communicating with others, elderly people included, and don't need instruction on how to do it. Others, though, are not so good. They need help. It is not a matter of smart or dumb. All of us are better at some things and not so good at others. Unfortunately the topic of how to talk to older people is too broad to be included here. There are works that specifically address this topic that you can find online.

Assuming there is no serious cognitive impairment afflicting your older person, you will probably find these conversations fun, interesting and informative. You might even want to record some of your conversations or take notes so you can share them with other family members.

After parents are gone comes the bittersweet task of sorting through their personal effects. You are likely to come across things that raise questions that, unfortunately, you can no longer ask. What is the story behind that old quilt in the closet? Where did the unusual clock come from? Why did your mother have so many travel brochures about Ireland? Why did your dad have all those hammers?

A good way to start a conversation is to show interest in the family's background. Ask a parent's permission to rummage around in their stuff – especially in attics, basements, and garages – to find things the parent can tell you about. This usually works.

What you can expect to find varies from family to family. With the advent of email and texting it will eventually become a rarity to come across, say, a stash of old love letters wrapped in ribbon. At the time of this writing, though, it is still possible. Your task is to find things like this and give your parent an opportunity to talk about them.

Here is another tip about photographs. Almost everyone has pictures from their past. But don't be surprised if you discover that hardly any of them are adequately dated or identified. Go through pictures see what kinds of missing information your parents can provide. Write what you learn on the backs of the pictures (in soft pencil; no ballpoint pens!). That information will be invaluable later.

Objects, too, can stimulate memories that lead to interesting and fulfilling conversations. It has been shown that even people with significant cognitive impairment often respond to objects from their past. When they see and touch (important!) something from their past, the wellspring of memory often opens up with a surprising amount of recall. An empty matchbox from the far recesses of the attic, an old tool found in the bottom of a box in the garage – any old object that played a part in a parent's past is likely to trigger a flood of memories once it is held and contemplated.

Lots of people have wished they had been told these things when their elderly relatives were still alive. You can add me to that list. One of my relatives I wish I had known better was my grandmother. I knew her as a somewhat unusual but very caring woman. She lived alone most of her life after her first husband died and did not remarry until she was well into her 80s.

I knew she was a terrific cook and had worked as a baker in a hospital for years. (Imagine, a hospital with fresh baked bread and desserts every day!)

After she died I helped clear out her apartment and found her recipes. They were handwritten in a small binder. I treasure her little notebook of recipes for what it tells me about my grandmother as a person.

Almost every recipe in her notebook is carefully written and includes information about where she got it. Hints and reminders are often included. There are the unsurprising comments like, "A few crumbs on top are nice" for a torte, or "very good" for her favorites. For her white bread recipe, after the usual list of ingredients and instructions for kneading and rising, she added, "while bread is baking have a martini."

That tells me something about my grandmother that I did not know. I don't think I ever saw her drink anything more than a little wine at dinner. Her comment about having a martini suggests a bit of sassiness and a sense of humor I did not know about. I am so sorry I missed it when she was alive.

She also inserted comments like, "Nothing is really hard work, unless we would sooner be doing something else" and "The 8th wonder of the world is wondering what will happen next."

With sincere interest and a positive, active curiosity about your loved one, you will learn how to make decisions about her life when you have to. And she will feel at least partly in charge for as long as possible. It will be easier for you to respect her wishes and to follow through with decisions about her care and well-being in the same way she would have made them herself.

Notes

[1]National Alliance for Caregiving/Family Caregiver Alliance is a national organization devoted to supporting families with information, support and resources. The Alliance is based in northern California but you can find state specific information on their website (www.caregiver.org).

[2]The Federal government funds Area Agencies on Aging to provide local communities with help to support older adults. Almost every state has at least one Area Agency on Aging. Most of the Agencies are combined with Disability Resource Centers to be Aging and Disability Resources Centers (ADRC). They provide a single point of entry to long-term services and supports. In more populated

states every county may have an Agency office. The name of these agency offices may vary but are often called Offices on Aging. To find the office in your community use Eldercare locator. Eldercare locator is a public service of the National Administration on Aging (https://eldercare.acl.gov).

3
Enlist family help

When the time comes for family members to work together to care for one of their own, roles and relationships will inevitably change. Things can get messy. Tact and diplomacy are needed as the responsibilities of caregiving impact the roles within the family. With the right approach you can enlist even reluctant family members to help provide the care that is needed.

As noted earlier, some families stay in the same town or neighborhood while others spread all over the country. It is not unusual for family members who have moved away to find it more difficult to accept changes in a loved one's functioning or abilities. Because most frailty progresses gradually, these changes may be missed during occasional visits and phone conversations.

Of course the opposite can be true too. Geographically closer family members may miss gradual changes in mental or functional abilities while a child who lives some distance away may be struck by the changes in a parent when they come to visit. Either way the increased frailty in a parent is hard to accept and each family member will deal with it (or not) in different ways. Denial is frequently the first response and may last until something negative happens. Sometimes it takes an illness or accident for some family members to accept the fact that a parent is no longer able to be completely independent.

In a majority of cases the first serious accident or illness brings children and other family members together, ready to take on responsibilities to support their loved one. Siblings who have drifted to other parts of the world to manage their own careers and families may find that the newly shared responsibility helps them reconnect as a family.

Even when everyone is on board and willing to help, challenges arise. Some of the first hurdles come from parents who resist suggestions for any kind of change because, to them, they threaten their autonomy and independence. Problems also arise when family members find it difficult to let go of, or change in any way, their long-standing roles and relationships.

Not everyone agrees that caregiving is their responsibility. It is not uncommon for one sibling or relative to have to take on the bulk of the load. Typically this is the child who lives closest to the parent.

It is common in most families for the oldest child to be the lead sibling. When they were growing up the oldest was a role model for the rest of the brothers and sisters. This can continue as siblings become adults and everyone tends to look to their big brother or sister when a parent needs assistance. But when one of the younger children lives closer to the parents, it is that family member who is likely to assume the lead caregiver role. In this role the younger sibling will have to assert more leadership because of decisions that have to be made each and every day. This realigns the relationships between siblings and can cause stress on their more traditional relationships.

Thus emotions can run high when parents begin to need help. Family members adjust to new roles and ways of interacting with differing levels of ease or difficulty. Some will find it hard to accept that their parents are getting old and will not be around forever. The struggle to accept the new reality brought about by parents in decline is complicated by several emotions. It is important to recognize and deal with them. Otherwise they can destroy family harmony and cooperation, and make it nearly impossible to agree on and carry out effective plans of action.

Fear, anger, guilt, and resentment are likely to arise in one form or another and in some combination. Most people will experience all of them sooner or later in a caregiving situation.

The fear of losing a parent is strong and shared by almost everyone. Increasing parental frailty and illness brings home their mortality and fear of their demise can be debilitating. The fear is natural but it must not be allowed to cause bad decisions about parents' care and welfare. Whenever a caregiver has to make a decision that involves the one they are caring for, the first question should always be, "Is fear driving this decision?" Once fear is acknowledged and brought into the open it is less likely to drive a bad decision.

Just as elders fear losing their liberty and their independence, so too does someone in a caregiving situation. Caregivers are often heard saying they feel like their life is no longer their own. Closely allied to that is the fear of financial encumbrance. Will the parent's resources be enough? Or will the siblings have to spend their own resources to provide the necessary care?

Caregivers can have real, and often justified, feelings of inadequacy. The demands made on caregivers can be large, sometimes technical, and often physically and emotionally trying. It is best to acknowledge such feelings and know that almost everyone feels the same way.

In some people and in some cultures there is a strong fear of disclosing one's emotions. This is often more of a problem with male caregivers in Western culture, but it can be a problem for anyone. This fear is most easily dealt with by disclosing it to someone. Not everyone, but someone who is trusted and emotionally stable.

Anger is another emotion hard to avoid, at least at times, in a caregiving situation. The two more common forms of anger are episodic and situational.

Examples of episodic anger are when you get mad at your parent for not cooperating, a sibling for not helping with something, or a healthcare professional for being emotionally obtuse. It is triggered by some particular episode and is not a permanent state of emotion. If you find yourself getting mad frequently it is helpful to have a little talk with yourself about staying cool, calm and collected. Try to anticipate aggravations and resolve to remain emotionally above it all.

Anger can take a heavy toll on you and everyone around you, especially your care receiver. It should be controlled. There are lots of anger management strategies available both online and at the library, so if you find yourself frequently getting fired up do some research and take control of your anger.

Situational anger arises because of more ongoing conditions. It is easy to seethe about things like being caught in the sandwich generation. That is, caught

Chapter 3. Enlist family help

between raising and caring for your own children while having to care for your parents.

Investments of time and finances can cause anger, as can being taken for granted by everyone else in the family and being expected to do all the work for nothing and with little help in return.

Guilt is an emotion that is almost impossible to adequately define, yet we all know it when we feel it. Some things make us feel guiltier than others and caregivers almost universally feel guilty about one or more of the following:

- Inadequate attention to or care for parents prior to the beginning of their current problems. Negligence that might have somehow contributed to the current situation.

- Care decisions that are made when you aren't sure your parent would have made the same decision.

- Feeling selfish, wanting to just get on with your own life, unwillingness to encumber yourself for someone else, parents or otherwise.

- Secret thoughts about wishing for it to "all be over."

- Imposition on your own immediate family for your parent's sake, in both finances and time.

- Wondering about inheritance and who gets what after the death of a parent. What will be left, and how will everything be divided up?

- Compassion fatigue.

- For being angry or resentful.

Resentment is a form of anger. It is a problem on its own and also causes guilt. Some common sources of caregiver resentment are:

- Time and financial imposition on an already busy life.

- "They've lived their life, now let me get on with mine."

- Other family members shirking duties and responsibilities, inadequately sharing the load.

- Inadequate appreciation or understanding from parents, siblings, your own spouse or children.

It is natural for negative emotions and thoughts to occur in demanding circumstances. The more openly they are acknowledged and discussed with other family members or people involved, the less damage they will do.

You and your siblings must now adjust to new roles. The stress of the current situation, combined with the uncertainty of what the future may bring, quite naturally leaves everyone feeling overwhelmed. The stress will intensify as your parents' needs increase and everyone has to contribute more time and energy. Coping with this will require open and trusting dialogue between everyone involved.

As an example of my family's coping my brothers and I established a pretty good balance. Each of us contributed different skills and time in ways appropriate to the circumstances. We maintained good communication and worked together in service to our shared goal of supporting our parents' ability to stay together in their own home. That is what they wanted, so it is what we wanted for them, too.

As the years went on and our parents' needs increased, this resulted in quite an investment by each of us in time, loss of income, and travel costs, coupled with the uncertainty about what would happen next. Each time a crisis occurred a new support plan would need to be put into place.

The one thing that was paramount in our ability to manage the situation together was our commitment to talk openly with each other and our parents. This allowed us to stay on top of their situation and adjust to their changing needs.

Fortunately, with the state of modern technology, even distant and busy siblings can stay connected. We found conference calls and video chats immensely helpful. Being able to talk and listen to one another's point of view and concerns goes a long way toward working as a team with your parents.

There are benefits for the entire family, not just your parents, when siblings, other family, and friends work together to help. Not only do your parents have better support but the involvement of many people shares the burdens of caregiving to balance the responsibilities and ease stress for everyone. As others help out, remind them to keep your parents' goals in mind as they contribute their time and energy.

Another thing that is helpful, in some cases necessary, is the development of a care network. The lead family caregiver will reach a point when it is no longer possible to do it on his or her own. When you reach this point you can organize a care network to include not just your siblings but other relatives and your parents' friends as well.

Organizing and coordinating a care network has three steps.

First, identify who is ready, willing, and able to help. Don't be afraid to ask and don't wait for people to volunteer. You will find that many people want to help but are hesitant to offer because they don't want to intrude.

Develop a list of the people you want to ask. Get your parent to help. It is best to start this while your parent is healthy and able to manage her life. Encourage her to think about her circle of family and friends. This is likely to produce a larger list than you would come up with on your own.

Contact each person on the potential care network list. Do it in person or by voice on the phone. Texting them is okay, but talking to them is better. Use email or snail mail only as a last resort. Your parent may also make the calls to ask people to volunteer to take on some of the things she needs. Keep notes about each person's interests and the kinds of things they are able and willing to do. Be sure to record when they are most available to help, like which days of the week and what times of day are best.

The second step is triggered when your parent begins to require support to continue living at home. Make a list of all of the things she needs help with. (You will have to update this list frequently as your parent's needs change.) Include things she needs at a specific time as well as things that have more flexibility for when they are completed. The third and final step is to match people from the first list with needs on the second list. Find matches between each of your parent's needs for help and the person who can fill the need. Confirm with each person that they can indeed complete their tasks.

Keep in mind that this process of creating a care network is difficult to organize until your parent actually needs support at home. Not many people you ask to help will be comfortable committing to supporting unknown needs.

Supporting parents' ability to continue to live in their home entails both small and large tasks. Who should they call when a light bulb goes out? Who will take them to the grocery store every week? If you talk to the people on the list about these kinds of things you might find a neighbor who is willing to make sure your dad's dog is walked, fed, and who might even be willing to clean up the yard after it. Maybe there is a nephew who will drive your parent to religious services. Is there a friend who will take your dad to the diner to have coffee with a group of retirees? As you engage people to handle the various things that need doing, don't forget to include enlisting people who can provide companionship through phone calls and visits.

Engaging others to help meet the responsibilities of care will change your role to coordinator, rather than doing everything yourself. Your parent may not be able to do the actual coordinating of all the people who step in to help, but do make it a point to include her in at least part of the planning.

One of the better models of networked care was developed several years ago by a group of people in the Chicago area who wanted to help support a terminally ill friend. The networking model they developed is called Share the Care.™ They developed a book and additional resources to help others follow their lead.[3]

The Share the Care model is best designed to care for someone with a terminal illness, but there are some concepts that can be useful in almost any caregiving situation. In this model someone outside the immediate family becomes the coordinator of the care network. When organizing a care network for an aging relative or friend it is more respectful for the older person to function as the lead coordinator of the network as much as possible. This can be done even if day-to-day details are handled by someone else.

The responsibility of the coordinator of care is to identify the tasks that need to be completed each day or week and to find the best person who is able to complete them.

As you work to find your own way to organize the care and support needs for your parents, the resources and guidance of the Share the Care model can come in handy. There are forms and checklists to help make sure your lists include everything needed.

Those forms lead to a lot of useful, helpful detail that is easily missed. Their task chart, for example, includes specific descriptions of activities. Cleaning is described as "spot cleaning, washing dishes, putting things away, laundry." Not only does this detail make it less likely you will miss something important, it also helps volunteers by providing clear expectations.

Of course your method does not have to be that detailed or specific. The most important thing is for you to figure out a way that works for you. You want to keep track of the care needs and who will meet them.

Caregivers often think they have to do everything themselves. It might pleasantly surprise you to discover friends and even distant relatives who actually want to help. They were just waiting for someone to ask.

Chapter 3. Enlist family help

Remember the *Caregiving in the U.S.* report and the average of 24 hours a week of caregiving provided by family members. With the need for such a commitment of time, it is easy to understand why tasks fall between the cracks in both the caregiver's own family life and in the life of the care recipient. You can fill these gaps with the help of others.

By the way, you can also find online resources to share the responsibilities within a care network. These are evolving and expanding all the time as older people become more comfortable using technology to help organize their lives. If you search for "using technology to coordinate caregiving," you will find numerous apps and other options.

Getting others to help has an additional benefit: It gives you emotional support.

An organized care plan decreases the stress that caregiving can generate. It will also reduce the amount of conflict generated between family members. A certain amount of conflict is almost unavoidable. That is just the nature of interpersonal, and especially intra-familial, interaction. But a plan and schedule will help minimize friction. If you find you need additional help navigating through the challenging of family relationships the 50/50 Rule resources for solving family conflict may be useful.[4]

An added benefit is that individual skills and abilities as well as time commitments are made clear and explicit in a good plan and schedule of help. When others help with the various tasks of daily life you will have more time to spend with your parent. That will help both of you feel better about the situation.

You should now be well on the way to understanding the things that are important to your parents, and to having a system in place to help you coordinate all the various activities that will help them live on their own terms.

The next area of focus is to learn more about how chronic illness impacts your parents and to prepare for care decisions that may need to be made in the future. It is very stressful to make decisions about care in a hurry, or in a time of crisis. Being prepared ahead of time, especially when you know what is important to your parent or spouse, will lower the terror factor and reduce the stress when you have to deal with a crisis.

Notes

[3] *Share the Care* by Cappy Capossela and Sheila Warnock. Fireside Books, 2004. (www.sharethecare.org) Provides information and tools to organize a network of care to share the burdens of responsibility that comes with caregiving.

[4] *Solving Family Conflict: The 50/50 Rule* (bit.ly/2HO4HvA) presents practical support for families who are struggling to manage caregiving together. It has videos and tips to help families work through the routine and stress that can arise in caregiving situations. Included is how to make decisions together and work through conflict.

4

What's coming and what you can do about it

PEOPLE LIVE WITH MEDICAL CONDITIONS that would have been fatal in the not so distant past. In fact, most older adults live with several chronic medical conditions such as arthritis, high blood pressure, diabetes, chronic pulmonary or heart disease, and asthma, just to name a few. If you learn something about how these chronic conditions typically affect older adults you can support your parents' decisions about their life choices even as their health changes over time.

As medical care improves, more elders are able to live a longer life coping with multiple chronic illnesses. In fact, most older adults manage these conditions for years with little impact on quality of life. But at some point these illnesses may lead to an increase in frailty that can extend over a long period of time.

Dr. Joanne Lynn is one of the this country's leading geriatricians. She is also a highly regarded champion for improving care for people at the end of life. In conversations with her over the years she calls this period of the last years of many people's life "the dwindles." The term may not be elegant but it is descriptive. It is the impact of several, often numerous, chronic medical conditions. The result is a long, slow decline in functional and health status that can stretch on for as long as eight to ten years.

The dwindles usually come on gradually. After each episode of illness or accident there is a period of treatment followed by recovery. The person might recover well enough but does not quite get back to the levels of energy and functional ability that he had before.

Pretty soon something else happens. A fall perhaps, or maybe the flu. Something. Again, there will be a time of treatment followed by a period of recovery. Again the person will regain much of his previous health, but not quite the energy and function as before. This pattern can continue for quite a long time until some series of events or a serious illness hits in such a way that there is no climbing back up. That is when the person begins to decline more quickly and eventually dies.

Of course this isn't the way life ends for everyone. Some people live relatively healthy lives until they are brought down by something like a massive heart attack or a traumatic accident. But more and more older adults suffer a period of the dwindles before dying.

The idea of the dwindles might seem depressing and unpleasant, but given that the alternative is to die quickly, most would agree that the dwindles is not a bad option given the two choices. When your parent dwindles you and she have time to prepare, time to share important experiences and thoughts, and time to show how much she is cherished.

You won't see the dwindles on any death certificate but we have all known someone whose life ended after a long and slow decline. Technical terminology describes causes of death as *failure to thrive* or *dehydration*. But in reality the cause was the dwindles.

When my mother's death certificate said "dehydration" and "malnutrition" my brother, Dan, was shocked. He thought that it sounded like we had not provided good care for her, even though she had daily care provided by compassionate home care aides with frequent visits and oversight by family members. Or, even worse, that she had been abused. In truth she had been allowed to continue living at home while the systems of her body slowly shut down. She died quietly, the way she wanted to go after a period of dwindling.

For an individual the first experience of the dwindles might be the awareness that he is no longer invincible, that nature is not going to make an exception for him. This alone can trigger withdrawal from activities and social connections. Some would say the experience of acknowledging one's mortality raises an awareness of what is important. Individuals no longer want to spend time with things that aren't really that important to them.

You might hear the phrase, "life's too short" when your mother no longer wants to spend time doing something you always thought she enjoyed. You might learn that she belonged to some social club, or that she participated in some activity, out of habit. Or because it was expected of her. But with her newly found sense of mortality she is unwilling to spend her time on things that aren't fulfilling or enjoyable, or that give her some sense of purpose.

On the other hand, withdrawal from activities and social involvement can be a danger signal. It might, for example, be an indication of despondency or depression. When older adults have difficulty coping with the changes resulting in increased frailty, they can develop feelings of powerlessness and loneliness. The result can become depression. This, in turn, can lead to further decline.

Some withdrawal and re-focusing on priorities is normal. But not always. Those who live into their 90s say that staying engaged with people and activities that add purpose and pleasure is important to their staying healthy. Understanding your parents better will help you to know if withdrawal is normal, or if it is instead a reason for concern.

If you see changes in your parent such as persistent sadness, loss of appetite, sleep disturbances, increased sense of worry or difficulty concentrating, these could be signs of depression. Be sure to seek professional help and evaluation if these symptoms arise.

If you and your parents are lucky and they don't die from a sudden illness or accident, it is very likely they will eventually become frail. They will become physically fragile and require the assistance of family or professional caregivers. As assistance is provided, the goal is for loved ones to continue to live as closely as possible in their preferred lifestyle.

To achieve this objective requires making the right life choices. All through life we make choices. When we have choices to make about our plans for the future, we talk with our families and our friends. We seek the opinions of others regarding education, job plans, dating, marriage, and plans for children. Prospective parents read magazines and books on the subject, attend childbirth classes, and so on.

But this advice and information seeking breaks down when people are faced with the challenges of aging. They tend to spend little to no time seeking out information about the experiences of others. Little attention is paid to gathering information about how to age well or to understand the choices and options coming up in the near future. The whole concept of planning ahead goes out the window, even when all their lives they have been inveterate planners.

As our parents get older the choices they make become harder and potentially more serious. For example they may decide not to take all of their medications as prescribed. Even with better coverage by Medicare, medications can still be costly. The need to buy groceries or pay heating bills might mean there is not enough money left to pay for all of their medications. In a situation like this elders are faced with a tough choice. Adequate food and heat are tangible and the results immediate. The benefit of the small pill may not be obvious so they decide not to take it.

One of the hardest concepts to accept is that if an older person is mentally competent he or she has a right to make bad decisions. If your dad decides that he won't use his walker in the house, you can talk about it until you're blue in the face. You can try to help him understand that walking around his home without his walker increases his risk of falling. But despite all your logic, reasoning and harangue he still refuses to use it. He leaves it idle by the door, "Where it belongs," he says. "I don't need it."

If you can get him to see that walking without his walker puts his goals at risk, you will be more successful. Suppose your dad has a goal to stay independent in his home near where his friend lives. You can use this goal to point out the importance of avoiding injury from a fall. But, ultimately, it is still his decision.

Some families find it easy to talk about the goals, choices and preferences in preparation for the last years of a loved one's life. Actually, though, it is more often the case that either you or your parents avoid this conversation. Knowing it *should* happen does not mean that it will.

Keep in mind that this is not a discussion you have once and then you are done with it. It has to evolve. Once initiated, allowing it to evolve naturally and slowly takes away some of the dread about having it. Most people are relieved to know that not everything has to be covered in one conversation. Nor do you have to get everything right. Several shorter sessions about the things that are important in your parent's life make the conversation easier.

With some people it is smart to get "mulled familiarity" working for you. This actually involves two principles of human thinking and interaction. First is the mull factor. Conversations and their topics leave a residue of thought that continues in a person's thinking. He mulls it over, sometimes quite a bit, after the conversation has ended. This has the benefit of removing the strangeness of the topic and leads to further thoughts about it.

Mulling over a subject also makes it more familiar, and familiarity can take much of the sting out of a subject that one finds threatening. It should go without saying that any discussion that has any relationship to mortality can be threatening. A gradual, multi-session approach spread out over, say, several weeks, can make it easier to deal with. For everyone.

Don't discount the importance of goals. Everyone has them. Even people at 100 years of age still state their goals. In fact in several studies of the very old, centenarians show that goals continue to contribute to a positive attitude about life. As people get older the goals may become smaller but they are still important. Examples of goals held by the very old might be things like being able to attend a graduation of a great grandchild, celebrate a wedding anniversary, or watch the Super Bowl. Something to look forward to or something to strive to attain adds meaning to daily life.

To improve your knowledge about your parents' goals, learn how they want to live their last years. When people consider the kinds of medical treatments they might want in the future and at the end of life this is called advance care planning. This will be covered later, but first, consider other preferences in order to have an adequate advanced plan for daily life.

Talk with your parents about where they want to live for the rest of their lives. For some, staying in the house where their family memories were created is more important than anything else. Others, though, might want to be freed from worries about the ongoing obligations of independent living, like mowing the grass or fixing a leaky faucet.

Some older adults would prefer to move but don't know how to bring up the idea with their children. They might be worried that their children would be upset if they did not have their childhood home to visit. You need to know about things like this, so get your parents thoughts and goals out on the table. That will make everything a lot easier in the long run.

Your goal, as your parent's champion, is to prevent having him become a faceless patient in the eyes of those who provide care at home, or in any care or living setting. Later I will discuss steps to guide conversations to make an advanced care plan for medical care, but first here are some things to consider to plan for life preferences.

- Are there limitations that affect your mother's ability to complete daily living tasks? Like a stiff knee or poor vision, something that makes some activities difficult?

- What is your mother's typical daily routine? What time does she like to get up in the morning. What time does she typically go to bed? Does she nap during the day?

- How often does she eat during the day? What are her favorite foods or beverages?

- What are her preferences for hygiene and dressing? How often does she take a shower or bath? Which does she prefer, bath or shower?

- What are her social preferences? Does she want time alone or would she rather be around other people? If both parents are still together, which is more important: living together or staying in their home?

- Is your parent's hearing a problem? Does she avoid social situations, like going out to eat, because she cannot hear conversation in a noisy setting?

- What kinds of daily activities does she like? Does she have hobbies or other preferred activities? Does she like music? What kind? What does she typically watch on television?

- What are the things that bring her pleasure or that annoy her?

You should know all these things, and more, because there is likely to come a time when you need to advocate and speak for your parent.

Life-affecting decisions are hard to make anytime. Making them for a parent can be especially difficult. But hard as they are to make, you will want to do this for your parents. And you will want to be as certain as you can be that you are making the right decisions. For that, instead of flying by the seat of the pants, make it your business to learn your parents' likes, dislikes, preferences and routines while you can. Later might be too late.

If your parent has impaired hearing or vision it might be difficult for her to adequately consider and understand options related to life and medical treatment decisions. Cognitive loss will also make this difficult. These limitations don't diminish her desire to continue making her own decisions, they just present obstacles.

Consider, for example, a person with Alzheimer's disease who has a cataract. Historically, many health professionals would not recommend cataract surgery for someone with dementia. But now the procedure and recovery are fast and easier. So today surgery is considered for people suffering from dementia. Even if she cannot herself make the decision to have surgery, moving ahead may be the right decision if better vision would improve her life.

A recent study showed that having cataract surgery not only improves quality of life, but may also slow mental decline by increasing sensory input. It is not hard to understand why – it is intuitively obvious that a relatively easy operation that makes it possible to improve vision is the right thing to do, if the person and family can handle the aftercare.

The mother of a friend of mine has dementia. She has spent much of her life with a crochet hook in her hand, known when she was younger for her excellent lace work. The results of her work are no longer as skilled as they once were, but she calmly spends hours every day crocheting. If she developed cataracts her life, and therefore the lives of others in the family, would be seriously impacted.

It is often difficult to know when to simply encourage and support your mother's decisions, or when it is time to step in as her advocate, or champion.

You obviously will not conduct functional and mental tests to determine your mother's ability to understand and make decisions. But if you know her well and are alert to changes, you will detect changes that tell you when it is time to support her as her advocate, or later to step in as her voice.

It is normal to experience some mental decline with age. Some of these changes occur from simple disuse. Without the demands of work and other responsibilities, mental abilities have a tendency to become lazy and sluggish. A majority of elderly people experience what they jokingly refer to as "senior moments." Such lapses can also cause a scare of impending dementia.

Scientific data validate what we commonly observe in many elderly people: The risk for mental decline and dementia increases with age. Nearly half of older adults over 85 will show some cognitive impairment. On the flip side, more than half of those over 85 years of age are still mentally clear.

Decrements in mental abilities can occur very slowly. The more common early signs of actual dementia are inability to recall the content of a recent conversation, difficulty recalling how to complete routine tasks, or forgetting recent events. Your mother may start sending more than one birthday card to the same person. Or none at all. Many things can cause concern, like your dad getting lost on a trip to the store or your mom absentmindedly putting her knitting in the refrigerator.

Memory aids such as notes and reminder systems help for awhile, but the family might have to intervene and provide more support for daily routines.

It is not at all unusual for any of us to need help from time to time with such things as figuring out how to record a television show or configure a new app on a smart phone. But when someone has difficulty doing something they have done many times before, this could be cause for concern.

The Alzheimer's Association has developed a list of ten early signs that indicate someone may be experiencing early cognitive decline that could become dementia. If you have concerns about your parent's mental capacity take a look on the Alzheimer's Association website.[5] Included in their resources is a checklist you can complete and take to your parent's doctor to share your concerns.

Another aspect of considering your parent's plan for life is to think about *purpose*. What is the purpose of getting up in the morning if all one has to look forward to is when it is time to go to bed again. I have a T-shirt that says, "The Purpose of Life is a Life of Purpose." Studies of healthy elders, and particularly very old healthy elders, have found truth in that aphorism.

"Purpose," of course, can mean anything that is meaningful to a person. Like checking on a neighbor every day. Taking care of a spouse. Being a crossing guard. Whether big or small, having some kind of purpose helps maintain health and a positive mental outlook.

A daughter might think it would be a good idea for her mother to hire someone to clean her house to give her time and energy for other things. But taking care of her house might actually be one of her mother's purposes in life. If it is she will lose more than she gains by not having regular cleaning chores. It might negatively impact her so much that she has a hard time figuring out what to do with herself when she would otherwise have been cleaning house. Elimination of the need to clean house (onerous as that chore might be for her daughter) might make it harder for her mom to get up in the morning. She might also resent her daughter for *forcing* her to hire a house cleaner.

So take stock of the things that give purpose to your parent's life. Learn what they are and support them, even if they do not make sense to you. Let your parent hang onto what is meaningful to her and she will be better able to ward off the isolation and depression that afflict so many elderly people. To have even a very small purpose will improve your parent's sense of wellbeing. It will help you, too, because your elder will have something to talk about.

A loss of purpose can be one of the biggest contributors to both mental and physical decline when an older person moves into a senior living facility. The days may be full of activities and there may be lots of people around, but everything is planned for them and that takes away all sense of purpose.

There are people working to change the regimented and totally planned way of senior care. One of them is a friend of mine, Carter Catlett Williams. She co-founded the Pioneer Network in Rochester, New York, which is a national movement working to change the way aging services are provided. The Network began with a focus on improving life in nursing homes. It has expanded to all places where older adults receive care.

The idea is to give older adults more say in the way they live. Participating care agencies and facilities use older adult input to change the way services are provided, the structure of the buildings, and even the way healthcare workers interact with the older adults.

Carter moved to a senior living complex when she was about 90. Soon after she spoke via satellite to people attending the annual meeting of the Pioneer Network. In her talk she questioned the existence of single-age housing for older adults and referred to her new situation as living in a ghetto with a homogeneous group of fragile, gray-haired people. She said there were lots of programs to keep the residents busy during the day, but very few of the programs contributed to any sense of meaningful living.

As she put it, "In our younger years, we live. We don't go to *programs*. We have *purpose*." She asked the audience to consider the difference between programs and purpose. And she challenged them to consider how to provide opportunities to continue living with meaning and purpose.

Too often families and home care services turn even the private homes of frail, older adults into institution-like settings. I think Carter's words are important for anyone helping an older person in the final years of life, regardless of where she lives.

It may seem like you are being caring and loving to make the decisions about all aspects of your mother's life. But remember this: The more you take over, the more you have to take over. Because you create even more dependency. Agency is like muscle fiber. It weakens with disuse. Anyone's self-sufficiency and functional ability will decline if everything is done for them.

Some people become passive as they age and willingly hand decision-making over to someone else. But it is more often the case that decision-making is wrested from the elder. It begins innocently enough. A spouse, son or daughter just starts to take over some decisions. This gradually grows until one day the older adult finds he no longer has a say in his life. The result is dependence, depression, frustration and withdrawal.

Doing and taking care of everything for your mother disrespects her. It is detrimental to her state of mind, of her sense of who she is. Besides, you will become physically and emotionally exhausted from carrying the load yourself. You will probably also harbor resentment over the added burden in your already too-busy life. Avoid this. Keep your parent involved in the decisions that need to be made, at the highest level she can handle. This will help her maintain her sense of purpose.

If your parent is experiencing some cognitive decline, or you need to change a pattern of decision-making you have already begun, start small. Instead of, "here are your clothes for today," try, "would you like to wear the blue shirt or the yellow?" Instead of choosing all her groceries for her, ask, "what can I get you at the store this week?"

Keep in mind that the daily living choices for older adults, especially as they become frail, are often made for them according to *what is most convenient for the caregiver*. Your schedule is of course important. But try to involve your elder in scheduling whenever possible.

For instance, you may drive your father to his medical appointments. Compatibility with your schedule is important, but you could still ask him about the dates and times that work best for him before actually scheduling the appointments. Maybe he would prefer an afternoon appointment because he feels better in the afternoon, or because he doesn't like to get up early in the morning. Accommodate his wishes whenever possible.

There is an inherent conflict showing respect for choice, on the one hand, questions of safety and wellbeing on the other. As a caregiver you want to protect your parents, keep them safe and reduce their risk to a minimum. How can you do that and let them make what might be risky decisions on their own? The next chapter has some ways to help balance these concerns.

Notes

[5] Alzheimer's Association, *Know the 10 Signs – Early Detection Matters*. Checklist to identify memory changes and the ability to complete familiar tasks. (Go to bit.ly/2Jy306r to get a copy of their checklist that you can complete and take to your parents doctor)

5
When staying at home beats moving

MORE THAN EIGHT OUT OF TEN older adults say they want to stay in their own homes. Yet almost every conversation about taking care of older adults seems to focus on one question: How can I convince them to move to a safer place?

But what is "safer"? Adult children worry that their parent will fall at home or do something else that endangers them. Falling is a real concern because most falls *do* occur in the home. Well, of course they do. It is because that is where most older people spend the majority of their time.

Moving somewhere else is not a guarantee that your parent won't fall. Statistics show that, per capita, there are actually more falls in assisted living and nursing homes than in private homes.

So, moving Mom to a place where there is 24 hour staff may not be the solution if the goal is to prevent a fall. Before you consider convincing your parent to move there are so many things to think about beyond your concerns about her safety. Moving away from what your parent thinks of as home has consequences.

Home is where memories were made and where possessions, accumulated over a lifetime, are stored. It is where neighbors are known and even the mail person is a familiar face. It is where friends and relatives stop by to visit.

Moving somewhere else means getting rid of possessions, often paring down to essentials. If your parent makes this decision herself it will be less painful, but still not easy to give up what is familiar and comfortable about home. A younger person may be able to adjust to a new home in a matter of weeks, while an older person may never adjust to a new home.

On the other hand, many homes are not well designed to *age in place* and moving may be a step that is important to make. Older homes, mobile homes, and even suburban family homes are often not well designed for an older person who is unable to easily climb stairs. Some adaptations may be possible to make the home more livable, but sometimes moving is the best option when all the pros and cons are considered.

But for others, living in a setting where they can interact with other people might be more important. Understanding your parents' goals regarding where they live is an important step toward understanding how you can support them.

Keep in mind your mother and father may not agree on the same goal. Maybe your father wants to get away from the demands of maintaining a house, but your mother wants to stay where the family's memories are strong and she has more control over their day-to-day lives.

Most people find it difficult to consider housing options. Staying put always seems easier than moving to someplace unknown. Your goal is to support your parents' wishes, while at the same time helping them minimize their risks. If moving is the answer to reduced risk, the decision will be most successful if it is theirs.

Wanting to stay at home for the rest of a person's life does not necessarily mean wanting to stay in the same house where the person lived for many years, perhaps even most of their adult life. If an older person voluntarily moves in with you, or to a condo, senior apartment, or an assisted living facility, the new residence can become home. The point is, what someone calls "home" can change and still keep the sense of familiarity, autonomy, and connection to social supports. This is especially true when a move is within a close geographic area.

We think of people retiring to Florida, Arizona or some warm place in the South, but in truth most people stay put in the same community where they lived before retirement. Unfortunately, many times that also means staying in houses that were not designed to accommodate elderly frailty. Such dwellings make it hard to continue living in them in old age or with health challenges.

If staying at home is one of your parents' goals you can start with a look around the house. If your parent's home is thirty years old or more it may need modifications or repairs to make it safer.

Some older homes are very difficult to adapt. They were built with stair steps inside and out, narrow hallways, tight corners and crowded bathrooms. Even when the home is not that old it was probably primarily designed for the activities of a growing family, not older adults. For instance, some homes have difficult approaches to the front door caused by entry steps that are spread out in an aesthetically pleasing way. They are pretty but quite impractical for anyone using a walker or cane.

Start with how you enter the house. Are there steps? Is there a railing? Could a railing be added? Moving inside, does the house have multiple levels, perhaps a step or two down to a family room, steps to a front entry, perhaps laundry setup in the basement? These are just a few of the potential obstacles to safely aging in place.

Many houses are built without a bedroom or full bathroom on the main floor. There are usually things that can be done to make a home more age-friendly. It might work to convert the dining room into a bedroom. If the only bathroom is upstairs, maybe there is a powder room on the main floor that could be enlarged for better access, perhaps even a shower added.

Creative use of space may be needed to support this decision so that your parents' home is as safe and practical as possible. That will probably mean more than just removing treacherous throw rugs.

Home improvement projects might include adding grab bars in a bathroom or installing a railing by the steps at an entry door. In some circumstances a ramp is a good idea. Before installing either railings or a ramp, or hiring someone to do it, take the time to learn how to correctly make the alterations or additions. Just like everything else, there is a right and a wrong way to do these things.

Railing should be made from sturdy materials and attached firmly to the house or ground to prevent a slip or fall when it is grabbed with urgent intent. A ramp should be stable, made of strong material. The slope should be gentle, with a rise of one inch for every foot in length. If the house has very many steps this could result in the need for a very long ramp, which can cause other problems.

Sometimes families add a ramp quickly, just to get one in place, but it is not made well and lacks stability.

The result is that, although an older person can walk up the ramp with a walker, it is dangerous without someone there to provide a steadying hand. The desired independence has not been gained.

If you and your parents want to make the changes around their home to make life there safer you can find numerous resources online. The standards of universal design provides guidance to modify living spaces to make them usable regardless of disability.[6] Even though the Americans with Disabilities Act (ADA) defines standards for public spaces their guidelines are useful for home modification because they provide such things as the height of grab bars and the reinforcement needed in a wall before installing them.[7]

Be aware, though, that many handymen or contractors do not have the necessary knowledge and experience to make ADA qualified modifications. A little preparation about this can be important to be sure the improvement is actually a safe improvement.

You can find many other websites offered by the trades that provide drawings and instructions. In some communities you can find people in construction who have completed special training for building to support aging in place. The National Association for Home Builders provides training and certification for people in construction. Those who complete this training are Certified Aging-in-Place Specialists (also called CAPS). Their knowledge and skills can help your parents decide what needs to be done to modify their home to make it easier to live there safely.

Another helpful resource for aging in place is the Home Safety Self-Assessment Tool (HSSAT). It is easy to use and does not require any special skills or knowledge.

It is available online along with instructions on how to make improvements to increase safety.[8]

Safety not only applies to the home itself but also to where the house is located. Some older people are set on staying in their home even though their urban neighborhood had become run down. It is no longer a place full of vitality with neighbors who know each other, but rather a neighborhood filled with strangers, noise, or sometimes gangs. It could be a neighborhood that has not been maintained well where walking has become dangerous and unpleasant from such things as broken sidewalks and other obstacles.

Or perhaps your parent's house is a suburban home where the neighbors have all changed to young families with children. None of them pay any attention to the old woman who lives down the block. Or worse, they complain because the house or the yard is not being maintained as well as others on the block.

In several parts of the country, groups of community members are working together to establish aging-friendly neighborhoods and communities. When they are successful, community leaders step up to take part in the planning and work to make it safer and easier to stay at home longer. AARP developed a tool[9] for communities to use to look at ways to improve aging in place, evaluating such things as accessible walkways without holes and tree roots, and adequate timing for walk lights on busy corners.

Perhaps the most important key to your parent's ability to remain in her home is her ability to move about safely inside her home. When she can no longer walk up the stairs to her bedroom, or downstairs to the laundry room, this can trigger the need for changes. Changes are usually worth it because they allow her to maintain her mobility for as long as she can. Universal design modifications for aging in place also help her entire care network.

Difficulty walking or moving around starts with a wide variety of problems ranging from painful joints to difficulty in breathing. One thing that is certain is that inactivity leads to less activity. And less activity leads to weakness, poor balance, and loss of endurance, making it harder to be able to move around.

The ability to move around independently is improved when older adults adjust their lives to add more movement in everyday life. Using leg muscles by walking more can be added to normal routines. To be the most helpful this needs to happen often, which means more than just one short walk a day.

The gradual reduction in activity that often accompanies old age needs to be reversed. It is not a good plan for your parent to spend almost all of her day seated. Recent studies of the hours spent by older adults watching television are astounding. According to Nielsen data, adults over 65 spend almost 52 hours a week watching television. I wish I could say that much of this TV on-time is just for company and background noise. But judging by how much people seem to know about current television shows, I can only conclude that much of this time is spent actively watching TV. Remember, less physical activity leads to even less activity.

Adding activity could start with simple movements like standing up and sitting down twice every time the person gets up. Like taking a walk around the house every hour or so. Even better, if able, walk around the block a couple of times a day. If your parent frequently talks on the phone, she can stand or walk around while she is talking. She can add a few extra reaches when she gets something out of a cupboard. While standing at the sink, she can lift up one foot and attempt to balance on the other. The whole idea is to move, and to move often.

The less your parent moves, the less she will want to move. The reduced strength, mobility and balance become significant risks for the increased possibility of a fall. Unless you are with your parent all the time you probably won't know when she has fallen, unless she is injured and needs treatment.

To emphasize the point, one of four older adults fall every year. One in five of these falls will result in an injury serious enough to lead to hospital care. In addition to hip fracture, head injury is the second most common reason for hospitalization resulting from a fall. In fact, falls are the most common cause for fracture as well as injury-related deaths.

Clearly, the result of a fall can be life changing. One of the worst things about a fall, a slip, or near fall, is an increased fear of falling. This, too, typically leads to less active movement.

As mentioned earlier, one of the big fears associated with falls is that somebody – a family member or a doctor – will decide home is no longer safe and it is time to move to someplace else, someplace presumably safer.

It is easy to understand why a slip or fall can lead to over-caution and less movement. But that is not the best solution. It might be counter-intuitive, but *adding* movement is one of the best ways to reduce the risk of falling.

Most communities have options available for older adults to increase activity, strength, endurance and balance. Senior centers, community centers and YMCAs offer low impact exercises, walking programs, fall prevention programs and Tai Chi. Many people find that they are more likely to continue an exercise program when they have other people to exercise with. But of course exercise can be done alone. It does not have to be with a friend or in a group. Whatever works is what is best.

To achieve the goal of supporting your parents ability to *age in place* you can also arrange for more support and services to come into the home. Communities across the country are developing more and more services and resources to help older adults remain in their homes for longer. Local offices on aging are always a good place to get information about the services available in your community and how to access them.

Increased availability of home care support can be seen in the rising average age of new residents in assisted living and nursing homes. Sometimes functional decline, frailty, or the lack of financial resources make it no longer possible for an older person to remain in her own home. Finding a different living situation can be difficult and time consuming.

Most communities have many options for senior living that range from senior apartments to more organized living situations with care staff, like assisted living or nursing homes. Ideally your parent will be able to be part of this decision. It will be even better if she is the one who starts the discussion.

Many children promise their parents that they will never place them in a nursing home. Nursing homes, even the better ones, do tend to remove the individual's personal sense of self and purpose. They operate with their own schedules and rules. Some of the rules are required by state regulations. Some are established to manage the care for a large group of people in a congregate setting in the most efficient way possible within an established standard of care.

Most of the care in nursing homes is provided by nursing aides under nursing supervision. Many of these aides are caring individuals but it is a challenge to provide care for six to eight different people. That's during the day. They have to care for even more in the evening and at night.

With the varied care needs of the individuals in their care, aides find it hard to respond to every need of every resident. Aides are trained for the tasks they are required to do. But they have little training to prepare them to help with the challenges of frailty, loss, and the end of life.

When you add the fact that there are three shifts over seven days the number of people who will be interacting with your parent would be hard to count. In the best of circumstances, where the nursing home works to focus on the individual people they care for, the staff might try to remember that your parent was a former French teacher and pianist, but many will not even remember her name and just address her as "honey" or "dear."

If it does become necessary for your parent to move to an assisted living facility or nursing home, your caregiver job is not done. Participation in care and vigilance to protect her wishes will continue.

There is a whole host of subjects that could be discussed to help select a care facility and work to ensure the best care possible, but rather than getting side-tracked we will focus on those who choose to stay at home.[10]

There is one more important topic to consider in regard to safety: Risk. Who decides when a risk is worth taking? It goes without saying that not all risk can be eliminated. Before you jump in and try to eliminate risk, it might be helpful if you think back to consider the risks your parents allowed you to take when you were growing up. This reflection might be helpful as you consider the risks your parents are willing to take as they approach the last years of their lives.

If yours was like most families, as you grew up you were gradually allowed to make choices for yourself. Simple ones at first. Bigger risks were granted as you got a bit older, like being allowed to ride your bike to your friend's house. Then later the first time you were allowed to take the car out on your own for a solo drive.

How do you think your parents felt about protecting you from risk? If you have children consider how you made decisions about the level of risks your children could take as they grew older? Most parents would like to protect their children from all risks if they could.

In recent years there has been discussion in parenting about helicopter moms. These are mothers who check in constantly and oversee their child's every decision. This so-called helicoptering is supposedly rooted in the belief that they know best and want to give their child the best life possible by protecting him from every conceivable risk.

If this is flipped around to the care of older parents, you should not want to be a helicopter son or daughter.

When you think about risks and safety, consider whether you have a right to tell your parents what level of risk is best for them. Is the real motive what level of risk is better for you? After they are gone, which would make you feel less guilty? To know you did everything possible to remove risk. Or to know you allowed them the freedom to make all of the choices they were able to make even if it meant they were at risk for injury.

As families work together to consider the balance of risk and benefit, keep in mind that a decision made for today may not work tomorrow when health or ability changes. It is a wise caregiver who has contingency plans for as many situations as possible.

Perhaps staying at home to age in place will work out for the rest of your parents' lives. But if something changes and staying in their home is no longer possible, you may all be forced to make a momentous decision quickly. Be prepared. Whatever it is, everyone involved, especially your parent(s), should work together to arrive at the best balance of acceptable risk.

Notes

[6]National Association of Home Builders, Aging-in-Place Remodeling (bit.ly/1NhRcfz)

[7]2010 ADA (Americans with Disability Act) *Standards for Accessible Design*. (www.ada.gov/2010ADAstandards$_i$ndex.html

[8]*Home Safety Self-Assessment Tool (HSSAT)* is available for download in PDF format from bit.ly/2rlTO9b. The download for screen reader users (.docx) is bit.ly/2If9uW9. The HSSAT was developed by the Occupational Therapy Department of the University at Buffalo. It is an easy to use guide to screening a home for safety hazards, along with advice on how to make changes to reduce risk.

[9]AARP Network of Age-Friendly States developed a toolkit to help communities plan. Included is a community survey to identify problems to be addressed. www.aarp.org

[10]For long term care at home and in care facilities, Medicare provides comparisons of nursing homes in your area. Their website contains quality of care information from every licensed facility that is certified to receive payments from Medicare and Medicaid. This site also has a guide for families to help with nursing home or other long-term care choices: bit.ly/1CHwbuM.

To find nursing homes or assisted living facilities that try to create an environment that focuses on maintaining the best quality of life, look for a facility that has embraced what is called "culture change." Some of the models to consider are members of the Pioneer Network (pioneernetwork.net/Consumers/). The Pioneer website is a resource for families. You can find information to help you ask questions about a long-term care service to find the best choice in your area. You can also find information about your state.

The Eden Alternative (www.edenalt.org) is another group that is working to change and improve the lives for those who receive long term care both in nursing homes and other settings.

6
Make medical decisions easier

THE PRACTICE OF MEDICINE is both an art and a science and has no set of clear cut criteria for making decisions in different situations. The decision-making process for older adults is complicated as they suffer from multiple chronic conditions. An individual's age, general health status and resilience can all impact the expected outcome from a decision about medical care. Care decisions are judgment calls. There are no right or wrong answers. But when you need to help your parents make decisions – and especially when you must make decisions for them – you want those decisions to be consistent with your parents' wishes.

When various chronic medical conditions cause functional problems to the extent that quality of life begins to decline, medical personnel will start to talk about choices for future medical care. They will ask your parent what he wants for care if there is a medical crisis. By talking about these choices and thinking about them in advance, decisions will be easier when, and if, a medical crisis occurs. Getting information and understanding choices is the first stage of preparation.

Medical care choices are seldom black or white. They are influenced by individual goals, needs and preferences.

Some people prize physical ability above all, while for others just being with loved ones is what matters most. While some might choose a treatment regardless of the risks, others might refuse any new treatment options.

There are many things that can be done to treat conditions that are faced over a lifetime. It is hard to argue that all of this additional care is always good. Sometimes additional tests, medications and procedures will cause more complications, more discomfort and actually just prolong dying rather than extend life. Sometimes the challenge for people who are frail and old is not when to do certain things, but when not to.

The Pew Charitable Trusts, a much respected public policy foundation, looked at end-of-life care in the U.S. They found that the care individuals received often did not reflect their wishes. More than half of the people asked said they wanted the treatment stopped if they knew they would not recover from their disease, or if they were in a great deal of pain. When conversations about these kinds of issues have not taken place in advance, treatments might be prescribed that involve unwanted (by the patient) testing and procedures that just cause more pain and discomfort with little promise of things ever returning to anything close to normal.

Some say the United States is the only country in the world whose population seems to believe that death is not an option. We seem to believe that there are always ways to extend life if enough medical care is provided.

People throughout history have sought ways to stay alive forever. Ponce de León's search for the Fountain of Youth is legend. But as we all learn sooner or later, no one lives forever. Perhaps what many people want is just a bit longer.

Chapter 6. Make medical decisions easier

Medical care can't cure everything. Sometimes it can't even relieve suffering. There are limits. When a physician suggests surgery or some other significant treatment, you and your parent will want to consider not only the benefits but also the potential costs and risks. There are always costs beyond those that hit your parent's bank account. Asking about the pros and cons of any procedure is important so decisions can be made with the best information available. Time and time again studies have shown that, when people understand both the positive and negative aspects of a treatment choice, most will choose the least aggressive option.

Some politicians argue for restrictions on Medicare treatments because of the large amounts the government spends in the last year of a recipient's life. In fact, more than one quarter of all Medicare spending is for care in the last six months of life. As more and more people live past 80 and 90 the cost for care covered by Medicare will continue to go up.

Controlling Medicare costs is an important public policy issue, but making informed choices for an individual's care is more about quality of life and balancing the benefits and burdens.

For several years a think-tank group of healthcare systems worked together in what was called the National Chronic Care Consortium. The concept behind much of the work completed was that the right care, in the right place, at the right time, would achieve better clinical results and cost less.

Unfortunately that philosophy has never persuaded the U.S. Department of Health and Human Services to modify the coverage guidelines for Medicare. For that matter, the philosophy has never reached any health plan. This forces difficult choices on patients, families and doctors.

Your parent has the right to choose and to say "no" to any proposed treatment. Medical decisions for a wide range of potential treatments could have different results if people knew all or even most of the pros and cons of the decisions they have to make.

As part of a project called *Sharing Your Wishes*,™ funded by the non-profit Health Foundation for Western and Central New York, an advisory group of physicians and other aging-care professionals requested hospital data to understand more about how care was provided in the final years of life for seriously ill patients over 85.

To pick the oldest and most seriously ill patients, the group used what is called the illness severity code. All patients are assigned this code when admitted to the hospital. The code assignment is based on standardized criteria designating how sick a patient is when he enters the hospital. The accuracy of this code is important to the hospital. It determines the amount that the hospital can bill Medicare for care given that patient.

To learn about care in the final year of life the advisory group selected several procedures for study. Two of the procedures they chose were hip and knee joint replacements. Such procedures are usually considered elective – that is, they are procedures of choice and not a medical necessity.

A total hip replacement is typically done because of pain in standing and walking due to arthritis, not to repair a fracture. Preparing for replacement of a major joint and being able to fully recover through intensive rehabilitation takes stamina and perseverance over a period of several months. The surgery is "elected" when the patient and

Chapter 6. Make medical decisions easier   87

doctor agree that this is the best plan to reduce pain and improve mobility and function.

The advisory group looked at the frequency of hip replacements for very sick patients over 85 years of age. This was considered a reasonable indicator of inappropriate treatment for patients near the end of life.

The advisory group found that nearly one out of every ten hip replacements for this oldest group of patients was conducted on patients who were classified as very sick and frail.

The professional advisory group concluded that, given that these patients were very sick when their joint replacement surgery took place, it was unlikely that the patients benefited from their hip replacement. They did not have the stamina to do the rehabilitation exercises that hip replacement patients must do. Frail and ill, these patients were at higher risk for infection and for skin breakdown, both of which reduce the positive result of the surgery.

You may wonder why these surgeries were performed. Sometimes physicians will perform medical procedures that are not recommended for very frail patients because the patient or family insists they be done. Sometimes medical procedures are done because they are possible and considered the appropriate action given certain diagnostic evidence. If a treatment is possible, why shouldn't it be done? In cases like this they do it simply because they can.

The group also looked at data about the kinds of life-sustaining procedures that were performed on this old, very sick group. The data reported that almost all of the patients who received artificial feeding through surgically installed tubes were considered "major" or "extreme" severity – the two highest categories. And nine out of ten of those over 85 who received cardio-pulmonary resuscitation (CPR) were in the same two highest severity of illness levels.

What this data means is that the oldest group of patients who entered the hospital in what was considered the most frail and seriously ill classifications were very likely to have intense life-sustaining treatments to extend their lives.

The concern, upon seeing this data, was that many of these older patients probably didn't want these painful, traumatic treatments at the end of their lives. But if they had not had conversations about their wishes with family members and their doctors, and they had not completed legal advance directive documents, then extreme treatment would be chosen. It is easier to say "yes" when treatment is proposed and difficult to say "no," especially when wishes aren't clearly known.

Chapter 8 will cover the most common life-sustaining procedures used at the end-of-life so that you can have a more informed conversation when talking with your parents' about their wishes.

The challenge for individuals and families is to learn as much as possible about treatment choices. Given the opportunity to make an informed choice – a truly informed choice – most patients will reject the option to have surgeries with uncertain, risky outcomes.

But medical practice is designed to solve problems, so surgery may still be suggested. Patients and families are given these options with the physician's "statement of possibility." Patients and families may not be given (or may not want to hear) all the facts about the challenges of recovery, so they go along with whatever the physician suggests. Sometimes it works out. Too often it does not.

If your parent's doctor doesn't initiate conversations to weigh the pluses and minuses of a decision, it's up to you to open the door for them. So says Katy Butler, author of *Knocking on Heaven's Door*. "The system is set up so that treatment after treatment will be offered until someone says enough," she says. "Doctors know this and may be relieved when someone says 'no'."[11]

A physician I know calls this the slippery slide of medical treatment. The system is biased toward treatment. Physicians are trained to make decisions and to act on those decisions. They will suggest treatments or tests that are possible in the situation. When they know these are futile, they may still suggest them because they believe the patient and family want them to suggest solutions. And then the family decides to agree with the physician's suggestions because they think the physician wouldn't suggest them if they were futile.

Just as it takes effort to stop someone on a slide, it can take effort to gain control of medical care decisions.

When considering a medical care choice ask the following questions to help you and your parent decide which treatment choice is right for her.

- What will you learn from this test that could change what you will recommend for treatment?

- What typically happens when people have this medical problem? Is my parent's illness typical? If not, what can my parent expect?

- What is the benefit of this treatment? What will happen if my parent does not agree to proceed with the treatment?

- Considering the age of my parent, do you think this illness can be managed to allow him continued function and quality of life?

- Will this condition continue to get worse regardless of treatment? What is likely to happen next?

- Will you tell me and my parent when you think she is approaching the end of her life?

One thing to remember about medical decisions related to chronic illness, especially as one approaches the end of life: Medical decisions are rarely needed urgently. You are likely to have at least a little time to consider the options.

When a young person is brought to an emergency department after an accident, families are thrown into a whirlwind of decisions that might save the person's life. But older people more often face decisions related to the management of chronic illness. The need to make rapid decisions occurs less frequently.

When you and your parent are considering choices in treatment think about an idea that was introduced by Dr. Dennis McCullough called *slow medicine*. Dr. McCullough considered the fact that most older adults don't die quickly, but rather spend months and years in what I have referred to as the dwindles.

Dr. McCullough believes that the care of an older adult should balance the possibility of improvement with the need to keep a focus on the person's quality of daily life. The concept he presents in his book, *My Mother, Your Mother: Embracing "Slow Medicine,"* is powerful.[12]

Dr. McCullough's concept of slow medicine means we should stop and carefully consider all care options to be sure the most beneficial choices are made. If your parent

Chapter 6. Make medical decisions easier 91

is too frail to recover from a significant surgery, then some other treatment option may be a better choice.

The idea is that, at the end of life, quality of life can mean doing less. At the same time, slow medicine will likely save time, money and emotional trauma for your parent and for you.

There is a lot of pressure in medical care to make decisions quickly, especially in hospitals. With slow medicine the doctor takes time to listen and collaborate with patients and families. The person, family and care team consider all of the options. The aim is to make the best care decision for the patient and her family given everything that is known at the time.

In the last year or two of life older people are often in and out of hospitals. They see one doctor after another, and endure procedures and surgeries that have a slim chance of making an improvement to health, function or quality of life. Just because something can be done doesn't mean it should be. The best care might be to say "no."

Saying "no" or "wait" is hard. You can be made to feel like you are making a mistake to delay or consider *not* doing a procedure. You can even have an advance directive in hand stating the patient's wishes, yet doctors may not want to honor those wishes if there is some treatment or procedure that could be done. Practice saying, "Stop, wait a minute, help me understand why this procedure is going to be done. Please explain the benefits of the procedure."

Sometimes the choices are presented in such a way that the family feels as if they must say "yes" to everything suggested. Trying everything possible is showing how much the older person is loved. But on the other hand, maybe not. Perhaps trying everything possible is causing pain and discomfort. Like I said earlier, it is not prolonging life, just prolonging dying.

The American Geriatrics Society (AGS) is a professional society composed of physicians and other health professionals specially trained to provide medical care for older patients. The AGS has developed several guideline statements to help health professionals who care for older adults.

One of the AGS's core principles is to encourage healthcare providers to consider individual patient values and preferences before making healthcare decisions. Their care guideline for treatment of older adults is based on five values they found to be dominant in the patients they treat. Older adults want:

- *Self-sufficiency.* They want to be able to care for themselves for as long as possible without having to depend on others.

- *Life enjoyment and quality of life.* They are interested in activities to maintain physical and emotional health.

- *Connectedness and legacy.* They want social and spiritual connections with others, and to express how they want to be remembered by the important people in their lives.

- *Balance between quality and length of life.* They want quality of life as part of making treatment decisions that are aimed at prolonging life.

- *Engagement in care.* They want active participation in medical and end-of-life care decisions.

Chapter 6. Make medical decisions easier

If you keep these five values in mind as you learn more about your parents goals and care wishes you will find ways to support them.

Healthcare professionals do not have all of the answers for what will be a successful care plan. They bring knowledge and experience, but they don't know the capabilities of the individual or the family. They don't know the characteristics of the individual's home. You and your parent bring these to the conversation.

The Americans with Disabilities organization has a slogan: Nothing about us without us. It is good to keep this in mind when you think about your role as a family caregiver.

Most older adults are capable of participating in their care choices. This is true even for those who have some cognitive impairment. They are often able to state their wishes. Later, when they can no longer speak for themselves, a family member can speak for them.

Your role to support your parent's care decisions may start as a second ear to hear the options for treatment for a medical condition. You may take notes about new diagnoses, instructions for care, or side effects that may occur. Later, you may be helping to explain to either your parent, or your parent's physician, conditions that relate to care choices.

One thing is certain: If your parents live long enough, one or both of them may no longer be able to speak for themselves, to make decisions about care. You have to be prepared to step in to make healthcare decisions, and very possibly other life choice decisions as well.

It is hard to emphasize strongly enough that advance preparation for these decisions helps reduce uncertainty and confusion when they have to be made. If you are prepared, you can respond to recommendations for care and treatment as they are presented. You won't be able to anticipate all possible decisions or situations, but if you have talked enough with your parent to understand what is and is not important to her, you will be prepared to handle the unexpected.

For the treatment choices you have to make you will weigh the trade-offs. How will the treatment choices impact your parent's ability to manage daily living tasks? Or manage pain, or have fewer side effects? Will the treatment extend his life by even days or weeks? What are the best treatment decisions to maximize those things that are truly important to your parent? It might not be living longer. It might instead be living better for the time that is left.

We do not have a delete or do-over button. We have to live – or sometimes die – with the consequences of our decisions. Sometimes we make good decisions and things work out well. Sometimes we don't and things don't work out so well. C'est la vie.

Each of us has one life story and what we are talking about here involves the last chapter of someone's life, his or her final years. Your parents have a right to say what happens in their last chapter.

Next, you will be guided through the steps to prepare to support your parents wishes for medical care.

Notes

[11] *Knocking on Heaven's Door* by Katy Butler. Scribner, 2013. A memoir about one family's struggle to combat the drive for technologically advanced treatments for older adults.

[12] *My Mother, Your Mother; Embracing "Slow Medicine": the Compassionate Approach to Caring for Your Aging Loved Ones* by Dennis

McCullough. Harper, 2008. Shaped by common sense and the belief that less can be more, slow medicine focuses on improving quality of life for older adults.

7
Your best friends
– *authority* and *guidelines*

MEDICAL TREATMENT decisions can range from self-treatment to the most complicated, high-tech treatment provided in specialty hospitals. The authority to make these decisions about care resides with the patient. But if your parents live long enough, and their needs increase, you will want the authority and their guidelines to make decisions in the same way that they would make for themselves.

Healthcare starts with self-care and self-treatment. It has been estimated that as much as 75 percent of all healthcare is provided by individuals and their families. In most cases this is the first approach to care and as you know in many situations self-care is enough.

On the other hand, though, some things are serious. They require urgent, perhaps emergency care which might include a 911 call for an ambulance.

But when the problem is not obviously serious, information is sought to decide what steps to take. Learning how to become more informed about medical problems and potential options for care will be addressed in more depth later.

At the initial level of decision-making your parent needs to decide if a new concern is serious enough to contact her doctor's office. If your parent contacts her doctor's office she can ask to speak to a nurse. She may also be able to send an email to explain her concern. Many health concerns of elderly patients can be dealt with in this way and need go no further. The nurse may provide guidance for self-care and monitoring of the condition.

But if the situation requires additional treatment everyone is launched into a different level of decision-making structured by the doctor and the treatment protocols established by his or her medical practice.

Once your parent enters care in a treatment center, whether it be a doctor's office or a hospital, the scope of decision-making becomes larger and vastly more complicated. Much depends upon your parent's frailty. As she becomes more frail, and especially as she nears the end of life, you may well have to make numerous decisions about all of her medical treatments. Later the decisions will be about life-sustaining treatments.

The preparation for some of the most serious decisions that might need to be made when, or if, your parent is no longer able to make her own care decisions is called *advance care planning*.

Selecting a healthcare agent

The first step to prepare for a time when your parent needs someone to speak for her will be her selection of someone to make medical care decisions for her. In most states the person selected must be of legal age as defined by your state. This is usually eighteen or older. This person becomes your parent's healthcare agent.

Chapter 7. Your best friends...

The healthcare agent has legal authority to make decisions as defined by state law. The agent is authorized to act through the completion of state-specific forms that are signed and properly witnessed. (See chapter 9 for more details on these forms and how to find them.)

The most important criterion in the selection of a healthcare agent is suitability. Obviously it is essential to pick the person who will do the best job in carrying out your parent's wishes.

Many older adults pick the most obvious choice without much consideration. Spouses pick each other until the spouse is no longer able to fill the role. Then the oldest or closest child is picked. When there are no children, or no nearby close relatives, there is likely to be more thought given to picking the right person.

The most important thing for your parent to consider when picking the person who will speak for her is to pick someone who will understand the choices that are important to her and have the strength to implement these choices – even if the agent doesn't personally agree with them.

Your parent will want to pick a person he can trust to both be available to speak for him, and to actually speak for him. This may not be the most obvious person. Your mom, or you for that matter, may seem obvious choices to your dad, but can he trust that you will make the decisions he would want, not the ones you want?

You and your parent might not have the same beliefs, values, and opinions about what is right for him in various medical situations. This might be especially the case regarding the use of life-sustaining treatments at the end of life. If so it might be difficult for you to serve in the role of her agent. The agent must be comfortable making sure your parent's wishes are met. If you don't think you can do this – and be honest about it – tell your parent and help her pick someone else to serve as her healthcare agent.

On the one hand you might prefer that your parent's death be with support at home, but your parent wants everything possible to be done. You may not like her wishes, but you know you are doing what she wants by following them and approving every treatment recommended. On the other hand, if your parent wants to die at home and you understand her wishes, you can make arrangements for care that will keep her as comfortable as possible until the end of her life.

The person who serves as a healthcare agent, or decision maker, can begin this role whenever your parent decides to transfer this responsibility. If she is unable to make this decision, the responsibility will formally begin when your parent's physician determines she is unable to make her own medical decisions. When decisions need to be made about end-of-life care, two physicians will need to determine that the individual is no longer able to make her own decisions.

In practice, a doctor will probably defer to the healthcare agent when your parent is too sick to make decisions, or if she has cognitive decline that affects her decision-making. Another trigger is if she becomes functionally unable to speak for herself due to a stroke or some other impairment that limits conversation and understanding. A loss of ability to make her own decisions can also occur for shorter periods of time such as during or after surgery, or when she is seriously ill.

Your parent's agent will be able to talk with doctors and receive all of the information about your parent's care and treatment options that would be given to her. The agent will be responsible to review this information and treatment options. The agent will have the authority to approve or disapprove the suggested treatments. The agent will also have the authority to decide where your parent receives care, including selection of the hospital, home care agency or, if needed, nursing home.

The healthcare agent's authority is limited to healthcare decisions. The agent does not have the authority to make financial or other kinds of decisions. If your parent wants or needs someone to take care of her bills, or someone to handle her investments in her retirement account, she will need to complete a power of attorney document to select someone to serve as her attorney-in-fact or representative. In some families the same person may be chosen to be both the healthcare agent and the attorney-in-fact, but there is no requirement that the same person fill both roles.

The designated healthcare agent is responsible for stating medical care decisions to medical professionals, but that doesn't mean the decisions must be made by one person alone. Siblings, other family members, and spiritual advisers can be consulted to review their understanding of a parent's wishes before decisions are made.

It is helpful if the person formally designated as the healthcare agent is someone who lives close enough to be present when doctors or hospitals need decisions. If the healthcare agent lives some distance away it is harder to assert authority in care decisions. If your parent is taken to the emergency room, treatments can be started before the agent arrives. These treatments may not be consistent with the parent's wishes.

Once an agent is selected your parent and the agent need to spend time in conversation to be prepared for the responsibility.

Advance care planning

The process of preparing for future care decisions, or advance care planning, should begin long before decisions need to be made. It will always seem like you have time for this conversation until it is too late.

Communities all across the country have launched efforts to encourage advance care planning conversations, yet most people have never had those discussions.

If you have had full and ample discussions with your parent about what is important in the way she lives her final chapter of life, it is easier to continue these conversations to talk about what she would like for medical care at the end of life. You may have discovered you can learn many of your parents' lifestyle choices if you just watch how they live. But to learn their wishes for possible future medical care or their wishes for end-of-life care you will need to specifically talk about them.

By discussing potential treatments together, and learning about the benefits and risks they offer, you will be better prepared. Once prepared, the decisions you make will be much less stressful. You will be confident you are making treatment decisions in just the same way that your parent would have done, if she had been able to speak for herself. Without conversations in advance families and doctors don't know whether to pursue heroic measures or not.

Most parents erroneously assume their children know what they want for care without talking about it. In one study it was found that almost half of the older parents asked had named a child to make these decisions but few had told the child they had been chosen for that role. The parent just assumed the child would be willing to serve in that capacity and would know what care the parent would want.

If parents name a child to speak for them, but the child doesn't know this plan, this is a set up for some difficult times ahead. Without guidance the adult child will be unable to follow the wishes of the parent except by guessing.

This is not something that will go away if ignored. As your parent gets closer to the end of her life it is almost a given that she will need someone to make medical decisions for her. At least three out of four people need someone to make at least some of their medical decisions in the last year of life.

Ask your parents if they would prefer to die at home or in a hospital. The first surprise might be that they are much more willing to discuss dying than you are. The second might be how strongly they feel about dying at home. That is what most older adults prefer. Yet the vast majority of older adults die in hospitals, nursing homes or other care facilities. For a small number of them that was their only choice because they did not have anyone to help them. But by far the main reason is because they had not had the all-important conversations that make clear their wishes.

Starting these conversations can be hard. Many adult children are surprised by the ease with which their parents can talk about death and dying. On the other hand, that may not be the case. You might hear such things as, "Everything will be fine." "We don't need to talk about this." "It is in God's hands." "I don't want to talk about that now, let's discuss this later."

Referring to the experience of others can be a good starting place for this conversation. For example, "I remember you were upset when your brother John died. You said you hoped you wouldn't die in the hospital hooked up to all that equipment. If I understood more about what you would like for care at the end of your life I would be more prepared to help you receive care according to your wishes. Could we talk about what is important to you?"

There are lots of resources available to help start advance care planning conversations. Your local medical society, hospital, or office for aging will know the services in your community available to help your family with this conversation. The appendix includes a simple guide, *Advance Care Planning in Four Easy Steps*. You can also look online for helpful resources including *Next Step In Care, The Conversation Project,* and *Five Wishes*.[13]

As of January 2016 Medicare allows doctors to bill for time spent talking with patients about end-of-life care choices. If you need help getting a conversation started, your parent's doctor might help. If you or your parent have questions about end-of-life care his doctor can answer these questions.

A group of community organizations on the West Coast developed a useful tool using playing cards. It is a card game to help prompt discussions about values. If you need a conversation starter, take a look at the Go Wish™ game.[14]

The Go Wish website allows you to play the game online. Game players are given cards with statements of personal values. The purpose of the game is to rank the importance of the value statements. If you complete the game with your parent you will learn some of her preferences.

Through this simple game you can learn, for example, that "to maintain my dignity" might be very important while "to have my funeral arrangements made" may be less important. Any of the cards can start a conversation.

Keep in mind that successful advance care planning is a dynamic process. Health conditions change over time so options should be reconsidered. A physician I know has her family revisit their wishes every Thanksgiving when the family is together.

While Thanksgiving may not be the right day for you, the idea of an annual review is a good one. Remember, things can and do change: Health status, family relationships, financial resources, and so on. Any one of these changes impact plans for the coming years.

Imagine the challenges when, at a time a decision needs to be made, it is discovered that the person who was chosen to be the healthcare agent died a couple of years previously. Or that the person chosen is available but had no idea he is to serve as your parent's healthcare agent.

Or that the healthcare agent has himself aged and become less sure of himself, perhaps has experienced some cognitive decline. Such changes are a bad sign in someone who is to be another person's healthcare agent because the role requires personal resolve, presence of mind, and courage. It takes courage and more to stop a treatment process and question any proposed treatment.

Health professionals generally believe most older adults are unprepared for aging, that they have not considered the decisions that will have to be made. When older adults themselves are asked if they are prepared, four in ten say yes, they think they are. Given the notorious unreliability of self-report measures, it is safe to presume many of them are wrong. But even if four out of every ten really are prepared for what lies ahead of them, there is plenty of room for improvement. Learning about the treatment choices that may well have to be made at the end of life, and having conversations about options, will go a long way toward making you and your parent prepared for the future.

As part of your advance care planning discussion, learn about the several life-sustaining treatments that are most likely to be treatment options. The most common treatments that might be offered to sustain life are:

- *Cardiopulmonary resuscitation (CPR)*. An emergency procedure used when a person stops breathing and their heart stops.

- *Artificial nutrition and hydration*. Procedures used to provide food and liquid. This includes inserting a tube to the stomach through the nose or directly through the abdomen. Also includes fluids introduced intravenously (IV fluids).

- *Mechanical ventilation*. A device to aid breathing when a person is unable to breathe independently.

- *Kidney dialysis*. A procedure used to cleanse the body's blood using a machine because the kidneys have stopped functioning.

- Other life sustaining treatments can include such things as surgery, antibiotics, blood transfusions.

There are pros and cons for each of these life-sustaining treatments. The importance of their pluses and minuses increases when it is the care for an older person that is involved. The next chapter will cover each of these with more detail so you have a better understanding of them. This understanding will help you guide a discussion about your parents preferences if any are recommended in the future.

Notes

[13] *Next Step in Care* (nextstepincare.org) is a practical, easy to use website full of guides to help older adults and their families manage the various aspects of healthcare with an emphasis on support through transitions of care from one setting to another. The website was developed by the United Hospital Fund in New York City.

The Conversation Project (www.theconversationproject.org) is a nation-wide effort to stimulate conversations about wishes for end-of-life care.

Five Wishes (www.agingwithdignity.org), in easy to understand language, helps individuals describe their medical, personal, emotional and spiritual wishes.

[14] The Go Wish game can be found at gowish.org. The game provides a structured and easy way to start a conversation about what is important.

8
Medical treatments you should know about

A GENERAL KNOWLEDGE OF THE COMMON life-sustaining treatments will help your parent decide which ones he wants and which he doesn't want. The descriptions provided in this chapter include what happens with each procedure and the potential side effects. In some cases the treatment will extend life and support healing, and in others the treatment will simply extend life for a little while longer.

The use of life-sustaining treatment has become a hot topic in recent years. The information provided in this chapter is enough to start the conversation but if you and your parents need more information there are many other sources to improve your knowledge.

Several books have been written about end-of-life care and there are numerous online resources from websites to videos. One easy to understand book is *Hard Choices for Loving People* by Hank Dunn.[15]

Another source of practical advice is a free internet site called ACP Decisions (acpdecisions.org). The site is hosted by a non-profit foundation with a stated goal of empowering patients and families with knowledge. A group of clinical professionals developed the site to help people work through medical decisions at the end of life. It has materials in several different languages.

ACP Decisions includes checklists and videos. There are videos on life-sustaining treatments and several medical conditions. Other videos provide information important for a variety of different decisions about care. Each video shows what actually happens with each situation including life-sustaining treatments. For example, you can watch how a feeding tube is inserted.

When considering preferences for care keep in mind that some of the life-sustaining treatments can be tried for a short period of time. For example, saying "yes" to dialysis doesn't mean your parent must continue the treatment. She can change her mind if she decides the treatment is not giving her the quality of life she finds acceptable. As another example, agreeing to a ventilator for a limited period of time might allow your parent's body to heal after a trauma of some kind.

Choosing to allow temporary use of some treatments will also give you and your family time to consider all of your options. It can also give you time to mentally and emotionally prepare for the end of your parent's life.

Cardiopulmonary resuscitation (CPR)

Cardiopulmonary resuscitation (CPR) is an emergency treatment to sustain the heart. It is probably the procedure people know the best, or at least it is the procedure that they have heard the most about. CPR is used when the heart or breathing stops, such as during a heart attack.

The goal of CPR is to keep some flow of blood through the heart and brain until more advanced medical treatments can re-start the heart. When an ambulance

Chapter 8. Medical treatments you should know about   111

arrives the emergency medical technicians will start CPR unless there is a *do not resuscitate* form easily available.

A person providing CPR pushes down repeatedly and hard onto the chest. Sometimes forcing air into the lungs through the mouth by a bag or another person's mouth. To work properly the chest is pushed in 100 times each minute. Sometimes a tube is inserted into the trachea, or windpipe, connected to the lungs. Electrical shock may be given to the chest and medications may be injected.

On a television show this looks easy and almost always works. A character collapses with a heart attack, the ambulance arrives in seconds, paramedics start CPR or use the jumper cables to restart the heart. *Voila!* The person is revived. Fade to the next screen and the patient is in the hospital, smiling and on the road to recovery.

CPR is hard to do properly. To be effective CPR must start less than eight minutes after the heart stops. A small fraction of people are restored to their previous health status. Many people do not survive. When considering the results of CPR on a somewhat frail person over 80 years of age the results are quite dismal.

Only about one out of five people who receive CPR will survive to be discharged from the hospital. The older and more frail the person is, the less likely the person will survive. In fact, for those who are older and who have chronic medical conditions, less than one out of twenty will survive to leave the hospital. For those who do survive it is unlikely that the person will be restored to their functional status prior to the heart attack.

You and the one in your care need to know that CPR is a traumatic experience for the body. Almost everyone who receives CPR will have broken ribs. Many will experience other damage including broken breast bones, bruising on the chest, brain damage, lung damage, and damage to lips, teeth and windpipe or esophagus if a tube is inserted. The older a person is the more likely they are to experience harmful side effects.

An older person is more likely to have medical conditions that specifically reduce the effectiveness of CPR. The most significant are heart conditions such as variations in normal heart beats. The best results with CPR occur when the person is young and in good health, and when CPR is started very quickly after the heart stops.

Talk with your parent's doctor to understand the risks and benefits of CPR. Ask about the chances of survival and what her condition might be like after CPR. It is okay for your parent to decide to take the risks of CPR, but it is important to understand these risks.

Now here is the bottom line of all this talk about CPR: If your mother decides she does not want CPR there are two steps she must take. One, talk with you and her doctor so her wishes are known. Two, ask her doctor for a non-hospital do not resuscitate (DNR) form. This is important because it makes it possible for your parent's preference to be turned into a medical order. This form will be explained further in the next chapter.

Artificial hydration and nutrition

Artificial hydration and nutrition are methods of getting food and liquids into patients who cannot eat or drink on their own. As a person approaches the end of a long decline and is in the final stages of life it is not uncommon to lose interest in food and drink. This can also be the result of swallowing difficulty which can afflict someone who is ill or very old. This naturally results in dehydration and malnutrition, so a physician might

Chapter 8. Medical treatments you should know about

suggest providing food and liquids through artificial hydration and nutrition. This means that tubes will be used to provide food and liquids. The procedure can replace or add to normal eating and drinking.

Sometimes artificial hydration and nutrition are an important and temporary treatment to help a person recover from a serious illness. This is a common way to deal with patients following surgery or during a serious illness when the person is too sick to eat or drink. In these cases the treatment can save a person's life while the body heals.

For those with medical conditions that make swallowing difficult, artificial hydration and nutrition might be used for years. The benefits outweigh the risks and allow the individuals to continue to live with their medical condition.

Artificial hydration is supplied by inserting a needle in a vein. The hypodermic needle is connected to a tube through which the fluid is introduced into the patient's system. It is called *replacement* or *IV therapy*. This can also be provided under the skin (not in a vein) with what is called subcutaneous fluid replacement.

Since our bodies are composed of more water than anything else, liquids are essential to sustaining life. It is a standard care for healthcare personnel to insert a needle for IV therapy in many different circumstances. For example, a person will have an IV started when undergoing certain medical procedures like a colonoscopy or prior to the start of a surgery requiring anesthesia.

In situations where artificial hydration is not enough, artificial feeding may be recommended. If artificial feeding is expected for a short period of time it will be done by inserting a plastic tube into the nose down to the stomach (called a nasogastric tube). If artificial feeding is expected to be needed for a longer period of time, a surgical procedure will install a tube through the skin into the stomach or intestines (called a PEG or g-tube).

Use of either a nasogastric or PEG tube has some potential complications, such as nausea and vomiting, and there is a risk for infection. Because there is discomfort during feeding by tube some people need to be restrained while feeding takes place to avoid injury.

While the person's life may be extended for a little longer, the treatment can cause discomfort or perhaps worse. A feeding tube can cause liquids to enter the lungs causing choking. Near the end of life artificial hydration and nutrition can cause fluid build up in the legs or lungs making it uncomfortable and difficult to move and breathe.

Sometimes family members will want artificial hydration because their loved one's mouth is very dry, however this isn't the most effective solution to the problem. Most people who are dying will breathe more from their mouth which causes the dryness. Use of moisture swabs, ice chips and small sips of water are more helpful than artificial hydration to keep the mouth from getting dry.

In nursing home settings staff will often encourage feeding tubes. This is typically suggested for residents who have cognitive loss. Families can be made to believe they are doing something wrong if they do not go along with feeding tubes. Frequently this is a staffing issue. Helping residents who have difficulty eating and swallowing or who have challenges feeding themselves takes more time than providing nutrition by tube. In other words, the motivator is for the convenience and efficiency

Chapter 8. Medical treatments you should know about 115

of staff. The facility saves money spent on staff time by using more feeding tubes.

One other point – in some institutional care settings it may be hard to stop use of a feeding tube once it is started. A religious-based care setting may not object to withholding a feeding tube, but they may have prohibitions against stopping a treatment they deem life preserving, once started.

Near the end of life, including when a person is in the late stages of dementia, it is normal to gradually stop drinking and eating. In this case artificial hydration and nutrition are not as helpful. The best approach is to provide food and liquids that the person is able to handle by mouth.

At the end of life, all body systems slow down. Lower fluid intake can make breathing easier and reduce swelling in the legs. Less fluid in the stomach will decrease feelings of nausea. Without eating or drinking, and without artificial hydration and nutrition, the person will most likely fall into a deep sleep and die within a matter of days.

Families often have a difficult time when they have to make decisions about hydration and nutrition. Even when they are following a person's wishes they are naturally distraught when it seems that their loved one is starving to death.

Food and meal sharing is important in all cultures. There are a host of individual values, social mores and personal memories all conspiring to to make this one of the hardest decisions any family has to face. When medical staff recommend artificial feeding it is hard to say "no," even when you know your parent doesn't want it. But this is exactly and specifically the reason for those talks with your parent so you have no doubt about their wishes, and you have documents attesting to that. This is not the time to waver; it is the time to follow your parent's wishes. You may find it helpful to know that people at the end of life do not feel hungry or thirsty. They will die from their underlying disease, not from lack of fluids or nutrition.

Mechanical ventilators

A mechanical ventilator helps a patient breathe. When a person is too weak and sick to breathe on her own a breathing machine or ventilator can be used to do the breathing for her. A ventilator is not a cure but it allows time for decisions to be made or, in some cases, time for the body to heal from some incident.

If a ventilator is used, a tube is inserted through the mouth and down the trachea, or windpipe, to the lungs. Medications may be given to make this process easier by keeping the person in a drowsy state while the tube in inserted.

After a few days the doctor will test to see if the person can breathe on her own. If so, the tube will be removed. If not, a more permanent solution may be needed.

This means cutting into the neck to make a hole directly into the windpipe. A tube is inserted into this hole. This is called a tracheostomy or trach. This tube can stay in place for a long time although the person will need specialized care at home or in a nursing home. Once the trach tube is in place the person can be more awake and will be able to talk. The individual may, however, find it difficult to speak. The insertion of the tube can cause damage to the vocal cords or the throat.

A generally healthy person may need a ventilator for a period of time after surgery or perhaps after a serious lung infection. The longer a person is on a ventilator the harder it is to remove it because the breathing muscles become weak and unable to work on their own.

One group of people who may use ventilators for the rest of their lives are those with high level spinal cord injuries that caused breathing problems.

A ventilator is like a crutch and can be a life saver. However, if a medical condition is becoming worse the ventilator will not prevent the decline.

There are fewer benefits of a ventilator when the person is older and approaching the end of life. The existence of chronic diseases such as lung, heart, kidney or liver disease also reduce the helpfulness of a ventilator. If dementia is present, the patient may not understand the tube and pull it out.

Your parent may want to use a ventilator for a short period of time to see if it helps restore her health. But accepting use of a ventilator does not mean she must stay on it for the rest of her life. Talking together with your parent's doctor will help her to decide whether she wants a ventilator as treatment. And if so, if she wants to put limits like a few days, or some other period or condition.

If your parent is having trouble breathing on her own and a ventilator is not used, she will likely die soon. Care at this point can shift to keeping her as comfortable as possible until she passes.

Kidney dialysis

The function of the kidneys is to keep the blood clean. If the kidneys do not work adequately, impurities will build up in the blood. If a person's kidneys completely fail this is called end-stage kidney disease. There are only two options to support continued life, either a kidney transplant or regular dialysis treatments to periodically cleanse the blood of impurities.

Kidney disease is increasing in this country along with increases in the number of people who routinely receive kidney dialysis. It is normal for kidney function to decline some as we get older. Catching the declines early allows for lifestyle changes that can delay further decline in kidney function.

Dialysis is the mechanical treatment used to clean the blood to remove impurities. Dialysis treatment must be repeated frequently, typically three times a week. Each treatment takes about four hours.

New technology allows dialysis to be done at home, in some cases, which reduces the time and inconvenience of the treatment. But home treatment is not an option for everyone who needs dialysis. Home treatment requires establishing a clean room in your home – without pets and plants. It also requires someone who can manage the supplies and equipment. The home treatment options are improving all the time but they do require the cognitive and physical ability to manage the machine and the fluids.

A recent clinical study of dialysis patients found that most older dialysis patients did not know that starting dialysis was voluntary and they didn't have to do it. They weren't asked; they just got hooked up. The study results demonstrated how important it is for older adults and their families to ask questions and express their wishes. A person's goals for their lifestyle can impact this treatment choice.

Dialysis is the right treatment choice for some, and the treatment will extend life. However it is not the best choice for everyone. Receiving dialysis treatment several times a week has mental, emotional and physical costs.

Chapter 8. Medical treatments you should know about

Dialysis treatments will lead to ups and downs in how one feels and many find the downs are not consistent with their wishes.

In some cases there are treatments that can support quality of life for older persons without dialysis. The best option, if a person is otherwise well enough, is to obtain a new kidney through transplant. A kidney transplant will extend life for years without the inconvenience and exhausting experience of frequent dialysis. If dialysis is recommended as the next course of treatment, ask about an evaluation for a kidney transplant.

Finally, kidney dialysis can be stopped if your parent decides that the burdens of the treatment outweigh the benefits. This can be a discussion and decision at any time in the course of treatment. However, if the person's kidneys are no longer functioning, stopping dialysis will lead to death. Medical management can help manage symptoms but cannot prevent the ultimate outcome.

Antibiotic therapy

Antibiotic therapy may not seem like a life-sustaining treatment choice at the end of life, but it can be. Antibiotics are used to combat infections caused by bacteria. They include pills but in more serious illness, can include injections and intravenous methods to get higher doses of medicine into the body more quickly.

Many types of infections, ranging from bladder infections to pneumonia, can be treated and cured with antibiotics. If a person has an infection that is causing discomfort or pain, it is hard to consider not providing a drug that could bring relief.

At the end of life, some people will chose no antibiotics. This could be specific and include some exceptions. A person may accept antibiotics for a bladder infection, because this is painful and debilitating. Treatment could result in very quick restoration of a better sense of well-being.

On the other hand, the same person may decide not to take antibiotics in the event of pneumonia. This would be a decision to allow the body's natural decline to death. Left untreated most older people with pneumonia will eventually drop into sleep and die.

As your parents and you consider the pluses and minuses of each potential life sustaining treatment you will see that no option will be perfect. Every choice has both risks and benefits. Once decisions about your parents' wishes and preferences have been discussed, the next step is to complete the legal documents that protect these choices.

Notes

[15] *Hard Choices for Loving People* by Hank Dunn, a hospice chaplain who presents advice and honest answers to help weigh options in end-of-life treatment decisions. (bit.ly/1w3S3X9)

9
Advance Directives – your instruments of power

ADVANCE DIRECTIVES ARE THE LEGAL STEP required to prepare for future medical care decisions. Preparing for healthcare decisions in advance is not just about conversations. Knowing your parents' wishes will help you to carry them out. But in order to have the legal authority to make their decisions and take action when needed, it is necessary for your parents to complete legal advance directive documents. The documents and requirements for advance directives are established by state law in each state.

If your parents do not take this step several things can happen at the time of a crisis. Most of them are not good.

Consider a scenario where your parent is brought to the emergency department at a local hospital. She does not have an advance directive document when she arrives. The emergency room doctor will not know her. Medical decisions will need to be made quickly and perhaps without all of your parent's medical history. In the absence of information decisions will be made according to state law.

If your parent is unable to make her own decisions about care the physician will seek someone else who can make decisions. In most states family consent laws (also called default surrogate consent laws) define a hierarchy of people who can make decisions. This starts with the patient's spouse and runs through several family relations.

Even when the family is present, however, problems can arise if various family members have different opinions about what your parent would want for her care. This can lead to delays in care for decisions to be made, or worse, care that is provided according to someone else's wishes – not your parent's.

If there is no family present, and there is no available healthcare power of attorney, a hospital may also choose to present the situation to a judge for a court decision.

Your parent can protect herself by legally authorizing the healthcare agent who knows her wishes and who will follow those wishes.

Advance directive documents are similar between states. However, each state establishes its own rules and designs its own forms. States may not accept documents that were completed according to the laws of another state, especially if there are differences between the two state laws. That said, if your parent is traveling it is better to have an out-of-state directive than none.

Following are some of the more common documents in advance directives.

Durable power of attorney for healthcare

The durable power of attorney for healthcare is also known as the healthcare proxy in some states. It is the most important advance directive document. In fact every person over the age of 18 should have a healthcare power

Chapter 9. Advance Directives...

of attorney form completed in case of an accident or serious illness and they are incapacitated.

This form provides legal authority for someone else to make healthcare decisions if an individual is unable to speak for himself. This can be either a temporary or a permanent designation. The selected person is considered the healthcare agent.

You can get a copy of your state's durable power of attorney for healthcare form from your local hospital, office for the aging, or many other community agencies.

Because this is the form that authorizes a person to make healthcare decisions it is likely that you will find numerous community agencies prepared to help in completion of this form if you need assistance. Some communities offer education about the use of the form and others offer individuals who will provide guidance on a one-to-one basis.

If you have trouble locating a copy of your state's healthcare power of attorney form, search the internet for *healthcare power of attorney [your state]*. There are a couple of internet sites that have gathered state documents for reference. These are the National Hospice and Palliative Care Organization (caringinfo.org) and The Conversation Project (theconversationproject.org).

Once completed, your parent's signature on the Healthcare Power of Attorney form must be witnessed by two adults who are not relatives and do not have any responsibility for your parent's medical care. If this document has not been completed prior to a hospitalization it can be a challenge to identify two adults within the hospital who meet the witness requirements.

Living will

A living will is a separate document in most states and not part of a durable power of attorney for healthcare. It is usually a narrative document that describes the kinds of care a person wants, or doesn't want, under various circumstances.

The Living Will becomes important when a person is terminally ill or unconscious and unable to make decisions. It can be used to demonstrate clear and convincing evidence of a person's wishes for care at the end of their life.

Some states consider this a legally binding document while others consider it a source of guidance for decisions. Since it is hard to predict what types of circumstance may occur in the future a comprehensive living will is somewhat challenging to complete. In difficult end-of-life decisions a living will can be helpful to show evidence of an individual's preferences to support decisions a healthcare agent is making.

If you decide that you want to prepare a living will you can find a few sources online with sample forms and guidance for developing a living will.

Do not resuscitate (DNR)

There are two types of do not resuscitate (DNR) forms. One is used only in institutional settings and the other applies to people who live at home and is called a non-hospital do not resuscitate form.

A do not resuscitate form sets forth and unequivocally states a person's specific preferences relative to the use of cardiopulmonary resuscitation(CPR) and other actions. "Do not resuscitate" means that no action will be taken if their heart stops or if they are unable to breathe. Both the institutional do not resuscitate form and the non-hospital version of the form must be signed by your parent's physician. With the doctor's signature on this form it becomes a medical order. As a medical order other health professionals are required by law to follow the treatment instructions.

If your parent has a non-hospital DNR form it should be very easily accessible. If an ambulance is called and emergency technicians enter the home this form needs to be easy for them to see.

Without an easily accessible legal document that says do not resuscitate, paramedics and hospital emergency personnel are required by law to use everything in their tool kit to attempt to resuscitate an individual in crisis. They will implement treatments according to standards of medical practice and the clinical judgment of the responsible physician. In an emergency situation, there is no time to have a conversation or to search around the house for a form that will tell them whether or not they should start CPR.

As was discussed earlier, successful resuscitation of older people is rare. State laws however are written in such a way that it is presumed an individual wants, and consents to CPR. The only thing that will guide a different action is when there is an order not to act.

In most states a different do not resuscitate form is used in hospitals, assisted living and nursing homes. If your parent does not want CPR it is important to have this preference documented in her medical record.

Some states also make available an official bracelet or pendant that can be worn to show an individual's wishes clearly. Be sure to look up your state's rules because such a device may have very specific requirements in order for it to be valid.

Physician Order for Life-Sustaining Treatment (POLST)

The POLST form – or the Medical Order for Life-Sustaining Treatment (MOLST) form as it is known in some parts of the U.S. – does more than provide guidelines and statements of preference for medical decision-making at the end of life. The POLST form goes beyond the DNR form to state which life-sustaining treatments a person wants and doesn't want at the end of life. Any special considerations including time-limited trials can also be stated.

The special aspect of the POLST form is that it requires a physician's signature. Except for the DNR forms, the other advance directive forms do not.

Because the POLST form specifically targets the treatment a person wants at the end of life, the form is appropriate only when a person is considered very near the end of life. Typically physicians will say that this form is for someone who would not be expected to live much longer than a year.

Of course it is not possible to know for certain just how much longer someone might live. So rely on your parent's doctor to advise you on when it is time to complete the POLST form.

Some states print these forms on bright pink paper. Again, you can make use the internet as your source for more information on the use of the POLST form in your state. The form varies a bit in name and structure across the U.S. At the time of this writing, only about half of the states have POLST programs in place. Meanwhile most of the remaining states are working to gain approvals to use the form in their states.

The POLST form can be important for someone who is frail. Once your parent has a signed POLST form you can prevent such things as trips to the emergency room for treatment that he doesn't want and treatments that have some chance of causing more harm than good.

POLST is not the same as a do not resuscitate form or a living will. In some states POLST includes DNR if the person wishes this. But the form can also show that the person wants all efforts made to sustain life for as long as possible. Also it is more specific and more legally binding than a living will.

Here is the most important aspect of the POLST form: By requiring a physician signature the POLST form turns a person's wishes into a physician's order. It instructs other medical and emergency personnel to implement treatment according to the preferences documented on the form. They are required to follow the orders of a patient's physician.

As more and more states adopt POLST it has been found that individuals who have a POLST form are very likely to have their wishes respected. And they are more likely to die in the way they prefer. If they chose "comfort care" they were less likely to die in the hospital and if they chose "full treatment" they were more apt to die in the hospital with all the bells and whistles in place.

None of the above forms need be notarized and they are not immutable: Your parent can decide to change a form or create a new one at any time. She may feel differently about her care choices as she becomes more frail or suffers a new illness. The most recently dated forms are the ones healthcare professionals will consider valid.

Once these forms are completed be sure to share copies with everyone who will be involved with making healthcare decisions. Be pesky about it. Make sure they read the forms and know what they are about.

It is especially important to provide copies to your parent's doctors. Once the forms are completed arrange time at your parent's next appointment with her primary care physician to review her wishes. Again, be pesky if necessary.

It is in your parent's best interest to be sure her doctor knows if she wants everything possible to be done to extend her life, or if she doesn't want certain types of procedures under various conditions. To repeat: If your parent's doctor does not know her wishes, the default care plan will be to treat whatever medical problems evolve over time.

Accessibility is key. Even if nobody asks for a copy, you can request that advance directive documents be added to your parents' medical records. Having access to the documents when they are needed is critical because they provide the legal authority to allow someone to speak for your parents when they are no longer able to make their own decisions about medical care.

Some states have started online registries so that POLST forms, and other advance directives, can be stored for easy retrieval by any hospital or medical facility.

Keep copies of the form handy so your parent will have it with him whenever he has a medical emergency. To make this easier, some hospitals will scan documents onto a small card that can be carried in a wallet.

If there isn't an app to store advance directives on your parent's smart phone, I expect there will be. You and your parent need to determine the best way to ensure that the form will be available.

Storing advance directive documents in a dresser drawer, your parent's lawyer's office or worse a safe deposit box means they will not be easily available when needed. They are legal documents but they are only useful when they are available to be used when the need arises.

Take a look at *Advance Care Planning in Four Easy Steps* (in the appendix). You and your parents will find this guide helpful as they work through the process of selecting an agent and completing the legal advance directive documents.

Keep in mind that advance care planning takes both the paper documents and conversation. Your parent and the person she has chosen to represent her as her healthcare agent share this process to help ensure your parent receives care as she would want, especially when she is unable to speak for herself.

But…forms and conversations might not be enough

A word of caution about advance care planning. You and your parents can complete all of the important steps. You can have had conversations with your parents. Your parent's primary care physician can have a copy of her advance directive documents. The advance directive can even be in your parent's medical record. But when a medical crisis occurs and your parent is taken to a hospital for care, the best laid plan can fail.

There are many reasons why a person's advance care planning wishes might not be followed in the end. For one thing the advance directive may not be easily available. This again points out the importance of knowing where your parent's documents are, as well as the value of sharing them with your local hospital and requesting they be entered into your parent's medical record.

Even if the document has been copied into a medical record there is no guarantee it will be followed. Decisions might need to be made quickly in the hospital setting and actions may be set in place before anyone checks the record. If you are there to advocate for your parent's wishes you can prevent unnecessary treatments that your parent would not have chosen.

Doctors have an increasing acceptance of the role of advance directives, but not all physicians easily accept the patient's choice over their own clinical decisions.

When your parent is in the hospital his care will be managed by a hospital-based physician who is not his personal physician. This physician is called a hospitalist. The hospitalist will function as your parent's primary care physician in the hospital. In most medical centers this will be a team of physicians who rotate to provide daily coverage. Typically these are internal medicine physicians. They are available during the day to see patients, talk with families, follow-up on tests and procedures, coordinate with nursing care, and facilitate care received at the hospital. By employing physicians to direct hospital-based care, the treatment provided is more coordinated and the risk for errors and delays in treatment is reduced. However, the hospital physician is focused on treatment of the acute problems that brought your parent to the hospital. The physician and the various medical sub-specialty physicians who become part of the hospital care team will not know your parent and his wishes.

So even though you and your parent have done everything right, physicians might ignore the directives for your parent. A hospital physician may conclude that either you or your parent didn't fully understand the benefits of proposed treatment. In such cases don't be afraid to go to the mat with the doctor or even the hospital. Use the document and be assertive to ensure your parent's wishes are followed. You may need to work up channels. Physicians in hospitals report to others and hospitals have ethics committees. Remember, if you have done it right, the law is on your side.

When my dad was near the end of his life he was taken to the emergency room after a fall. My brother, Peter, took Dad's POLST form and his healthcare power of attorney form with him when he was called to go to the hospital. Dad was clear that he did not want life-sustaining treatments.

By the time Peter arrived at the hospital Dad was on oxygen and had an IV tube. The medical staff told Peter that Dad was dehydrated and needed the IV and that his oxygen levels were low. Dad pulled off the oxygen mask and pulled out the IV saying he didn't want either of these treatments. The medical staff's intent was to put Dad's hands in restraints and to re-start the IV and oxygen.

Peter showed the physician in charge the POLST form. The physician wasn't familiar with the form and would not follow the instructions on the form without having Dad restate this was still his wish. This happened even though the POLST form was signed by my dad's personal physician.

Again, a demonstration of the advantage of being an informed healthcare agent who can feel empowered to speak up when the person's wishes are being questioned.

If Dad had not been able to speak up to confirm his choices, it would have been up to Peter to ensure Dad received care according to his wishes.

The care of patients as they near the end of life is changing but unfortunately studies continue to show that dying patients' wishes are not being followed in care decisions. When asked, physicians say they follow advance care planning documents when they exist. But in reviews of care of patients in the last months of their lives, many patients go through extensive and aggressive care even when their documents expressly oppose such care.

A report released by the Institute of Medicine stated that physicians do not trust advanced directives if they are a few years old. If a relative states the document is out-of-date and approves a more aggressive treatment plan, it is likely the physician will proceed with the treatment. The legal risk of being sued by a surviving family member is considered a threat. However virtually no physicians are sued by families when the treatment was according to the patient's wishes for less aggressive care.

A secondary consequence of the advances in medical care is a growing number of people who survive catastrophic illnesses and heroic efforts. More and more people survive care in emergency rooms, surgery and intensive care. While this is often wonderful news, it has also resulted in growing numbers of older adults who spend their final months, or sometimes years, dependent on a ventilator or other technology to keep them alive. These individuals are not able to return home and few nursing homes have the capability to manage their care, so they remain in a specialty hospital facility.

The decisions that lead to this situation might well be the result of following the wishes of the patient and be compatible with their values. However, without understanding wishes in advance, this can also lead to individuals being kept in a near death condition when they would have preferred a less intensive approach to care, when their choice would have allowed them to die a more natural death.

One more important reason to complete a healthcare power attorney form is to have the legal document that allows you access to your parent's health information.

Most people have heard about HIPAA, which stands for the Health Insurance Portability and Accountability Act. This law has been in existence for about twenty years and the procedures allowing access to medical information have become routine in most settings.

The law was designed to protect patient's personal health information. Only those who need to know the information in order to provide care are allowed to see what they need to know. When a person is not able to state their approval to share health information, physicians will often proceed to share information with family members, if it is necessary for establishing a treatment plan and the family member is directly involved in the person's care.

If you are your parent's healthcare agent there is no question about your right and need to access to her health information.

Sometimes it seems like the privacy act goes too far and can create stress by denying access to information that family members want and need to know. It is important to know what your rights are as a family member and as a healthcare agent.

An excellent resource that explains this law in language that is easy to understand and interpret was developed by the United Hospital Fund in New York. This resource, HIPAA: Questions and Answers for Family Caregivers, is part of a larger set of resources called Next Step in Care.™[16]

More about artificial hydration and nutrition

Whatever your parents decide about their wishes for the use of artificial hydration and nutrition, *their advance directive document must be clearly state that the agent knows the person's wishes about artificial hydration and nutrition.* In some states if this wish is not documented the healthcare agent does not have the authority to make this decision, regardless of how well the parent's wishes are known.

If your parent's preference for the use of artificial hydration and nutrition is not clearly stated on the healthcare power of attorney form, the inference is that she approves this treatment approach. The statement of her preference must be clearly written to state whether she accepts artificial hydration and nutrition always, in limited circumstances, or never.

If limited use of this treatment is her preference, this should be described as clearly as possible. This statement can also include the conditions under which artificial hydration and nutrition may be started and then stopped.

Discuss the decision with your parent's physician and ask about the conditions where temporary treatment might be beneficial. Some people will only want artificial hydration and nutrition if it could help return them to a better quality of life. A statement can clearly state the wish to allow the body to die naturally when the probability of returning to a good quality of life is unlikely.

Others believe it is important to live as long as possible even if artificial hydration may cause discomfort and other medical problems. If this is your parent's belief, it is just as important to make note of this decision on her advance directive document.

Whatever your parents decide, be sure this preference is written on their durable power of attorney for healthcare form so their wishes are clear. You may need to make this decision one day and you will want the authority to follow your parent's wishes.

Plan ahead? Or wait until necessary?

Everyone hopes they will never be in the position where they will have to make some of these tough decisions for a person they love. In reality, as you consider the likelihood that one or both of your parents will end their lives in a slow decline of the dwindles, it is very likely you will be called upon to make some healthcare decisions for them. And, before that point, you may be asked, and expected, to be informed enough to assist your parents in making healthcare decisions to guide their care.

If all this discussion seems too difficult or too painful you can decide to wait. You may believe it will be easier to make a medical decision when you know what it is. You believe you will be able to complete the legal documents giving you the authority to act for your parent at that time. In fact, that is what most people actually do.

While more people are completing healthcare power of attorney forms, it is estimated that fewer than half of the adults in the U.S. have done so.

But be warned that if you decide you can wait you may be forced into making decisions with no real idea of what your parent would really want. At such times there are likely to be emotional stress, time pressures (Hurry up and decide!), and disagreement among family members. These are terrible circumstances in which to have to make life-affecting decisions. In a medical crisis doctors cannot wait until members of the family have a well thought out conversation and come to agreement on treatment options. They will want decisions fast or they will make the decisions for you.

If you don't know your parent's wishes you will never know if you made the right decision.

Notes

[16]The Next Step in Care website (www.nextstepincare.org) is a practical, easy to use website full of guides to help older adults and their families manage the various aspects of healthcare with an emphasis on support through transitions of care from one setting to another. The website was developed by the United Hospital Fund in New York City.

10
Your best choices in your parents final stages of life

REPEATED STUDIES HAVE SHOWN that most people would prefer to die at home, mentally clear, with family nearby. They prefer to be free of pain of course but will often tolerate some pain in order to be more alert, in control and able to engage with their loved ones.

Few would consciously choose to spend their final days in a hospital, hooked up to life-sustaining equipment surrounded by noise, lights and strangers. Yet, without knowing preferences and having the confidence to speak up when treatment options are suggested, many people are subjected to this unnatural way of dying.

Nine out of ten physicians, when asked about their own care preferences, say they value well-being over just being. They would prefer to die at home peacefully rather than receive aggressive treatment to the end. Studies of end-of-life care have found that more than eight out of ten older adults feel the same way.

Yet these days patients are more and very likely to receive high-tech, highly intensive treatment in their last weeks of life. Medicare data shows that six out of ten older adults die in hospitals, often in intensive care.

Why does this happen? Families are frequently heard vowing "to beat this," whatever "this" has afflicted their elderly loved one. They ask doctors to do everything they can which results in tests, procedures, medications, time spent in ICU connected to monitors, tubes and other contraptions. Complicating this picture is the guilt adult children sometimes feel for having been absent when their parents needed help. Or perhaps they are driven by their own fears of loss or fears of death.

Ask yourself how important it is to you to be able to say, "We did everything we could." Or would it be more important for you to be able to say, "Mom had the care she wanted?" Will you feel guilty if you don't do everything possible? What if you ask for everything possible and your loved one experiences days or weeks of suffering? There is always some guilt when a loved one dies but you are less likely to feel guilty if you know and follow their wishes.

When asked, most older adults say they want three things:

- Doctors to keep them comfortable at the end of life.

- To be told what they need to know about their illness.

- Reassurance about the things that frighten them.

You need to know these things, these preferences of your loved one, and that requires talking about them. These conversations are hard and they take time.

Palliative care

If a person lives long enough to experience the dwindles she will likely have need for palliative care. The

Chapter 10. Your best choices...

focus of palliative care is primarily on comfort. Palliative care provides many of the benefits of hospice care but does not require the cessation of treatments (a requirement of hospice care). Most hospitals and home health agencies now offer palliative care services.

At some point the need for comfort and management of symptoms is more important than treatments focused on cure. Care needs will change over time with more focus on cure during a setback, or after something new happens medically. Care focuses on quality of life when medical illnesses are more stable.

Patients and their families often balk when a healthcare provider suggests palliative care. They are not ready to give up treatments that focus on potential recovery and extending life. But, as pointed out earlier, at some point continued treatment prolongs dying, not living.

Peace and comfort can come from knowing that it is no longer necessary to fight with every resource medical care can provide. That doesn't mean care stops; the goals for care are just different.

Palliative care is focused on relief from suffering which is something every patient needs. If you and your parent decide that it is time to change the focus of care from finding the next treatment option to a focus on relief and comfort, it is time to shift toward palliative care treatment goals.

Some people are surprised to learn that palliative care might, in some cases, actually mean more care. Doctors, nurses and other healthcare providers will provide more emotional and spiritual support along with medications and other treatments that are selected to ease symptoms. They also help patients and their families understand and evaluate complex medical decisions.

Typically the staff providing palliative care have more time to spend with patients and families to have these conversations. Decisions can be made with less stress. Those who have the benefit of palliative care frequently state their quality of life is better than those who do not have this care benefit, and they are more satisfied with the care they receive.

Patients who receive palliative care have better control of their troublesome symptoms. This means less pain and easier breathing. Because options have been discussed and wishes are shared, it is also typical that people who are receiving palliative care spend less time in intensive care units. Older adults who have chosen a palliative care focus will also have fewer trips to the hospital for emergency care or admission.

In truth we all want palliative care anytime we are sick. Soft pillows, a tuck of the covers, a calming tender touch of a loved one's hand all give us palliative care when we are ill or recovering. Ginger ale for a stomach ache and chicken soup for a cold are palliative care.

Over the past several decades hospitals have modified the design of their buildings and changed everything from entrances to lobbies and waiting rooms. There is today a more concerted effort to create an environment of healing and calm. You can see children's wings with lively decor and bright colors. Maternity units with designs that are strikingly feminine and homey. Everywhere in the hospital you are likely to see pleasing colors, textures and lighting. These all contribute to the palliative care of hospital patients.

As one nears the end of life it is appropriate and natural to have care more focused on comfort with less emphasis on diagnosis and treatment. The challenge is often when to make the change to palliative care.

It can be a relief to both the older person as well as family members to make this decision. When persons with terminal conditions receive palliative care early in their care they show better coping skills and a higher quality of life. They are more likely to take steps that improve their lives and to be more accepting of their diagnosis. The decision to start palliative care also makes it easier to have conversations about preferences for care and treatment at the end of life.

Ultimately palliative care becomes end-of-life care. When someone is near the end of life – when doctors conclude that someone is not be expected to live much longer than a year – it could be time to consider hospice care as a more formal approach to palliative and end-of-life care.

Palliative care and hospice care are not identical. Hospice agencies provide palliative care, but not all palliative care is provided by hospice agencies.

Hospice care

When a person can no longer benefit from treatment, or decides to stop treatment, he can be evaluated for enrollment in hospice care. To qualify for hospice care a person must meet Medicare criteria that predicts that the person is unlikely to live longer than six months given the expected future for their medical condition. If the criteria are met, enrollment with full Medicare hospice benefits is possible. Once enrolled hospice services are covered by Medicare.

That doesn't mean that the person will die within six months, and in fact with the full support of hospice many find their health condition improves in the weeks after enrollment.

It can be hard to decide when it is time to stop treatments, but on the other hand, many older adults are very clear that they do not want another trip to the hospital emergency department. When given a choice most people will choose palliative care as they near the end of life. In most areas of the country, this switch in care can include engaging local hospice services.

The National Hospice and Palliative Care Association has reported that almost half of all Medicare beneficiaries were enrolled in hospice at the very end of their lives. Sadly enrollment is often so late in the person's life that almost half of those who enroll in hospice care receive the support for two weeks or less.

Hospice care is team based and includes medical care, pain management, and emotional support. To enable their comprehensive care hospice care provides needed medications, medical supplies and equipment. The goal of hospice care is to get to know the person and family, counsel them through difficult decisions, give support when times get tough, and provide medical care to ease pain and discomfort.

In short, hospice staff members work as a team to help individuals and their families handle the many complex issues that can arise near the end of life. The hospice team not only treats the enrolled patient, they also provide education and support for members of the family. Family members learn how best to support their loved one and to deal with their own feelings and emotions.

The hospice care team provides care and support that emphasizes comfort and dignity. They are experts in pain management and can work to manage a balance between full pain management and alertness. It is not surprising that some people improve after enrollment in hospice as a result of the rich supportive care.

Both of my parents and in-laws had the support of hospice at the end of their lives. Each of them was able to die at home with support. The regular visits by the hospice nurse and social worker helped each person and family deal with the changes that occur as life ends.

Hospice provides reassurance that by not responding to every clinical change you are not being a bad son or daughter. You are fulfilling your parent's wishes. When a loved one is enrolled in hospice there is a sense that you are not handling the experience alone. You have a team of people who understand your parent's situation, professionals you can call any time you have a question or concern.

Hospice staff will review the medications your parent takes and gradually reduce or eliminate those that she takes for long-term benefits in prevention and management of symptoms. Not surprisingly this can actually mean your parent feels better, more herself. She will no longer have the various side effects she has learned to live with – those that came along with her long list of medications. As a person nears the end of life the purpose of using medications shifts to include only those that manage symptoms to enhance comfort and reduce pain.

Hospice teams do work with patients in hospitals and nursing homes, but their focus is on providing care for people in their own homes. Many people enrolled in hospice can spend their last days and weeks at home surrounded by family and the things that are familiar and bring comfort.

Some hospice organizations have small residential care facilities to provide more involved care when the demands of care become too difficult in the home.

People enrolled in hospice are re-evaluated periodically and enrollment can continue much beyond the six months of expected coverage. Each time a person is re-evaluated the same criteria used at enrollment apply. The clinical team determines whether it is likely the person will die within the coming six months. Renewed enrollment can happen multiple times.

Worry about what happens after six months is seldom a concern. People put off making the decision to stop active treatments and ultimately enroll in hospice perhaps only days or weeks before death. Families who engage hospice never say they wish they had waited longer, but many say they wish they had chosen hospice sooner.

Why don't more people die at home?

If most people would prefer to die at home then why doesn't it happen more often? Most older adults have multi-chronic illnesses. They tend to be unpredictable and that makes it difficult to anticipate how they will develop over time. The interaction between an elderly person's various medical conditions can make it virtually impossible to predict their health status at any given time.

When symptoms of a condition like heart disease get worse, or a person experiences some new symptom or problem, families and healthcare providers opt for hospital care. Finding a solution for the new problem seems the obvious choice.

Families turn to hospitals for care at the end of life when there is a need for more constant care. It may be necessary for a person at the end of life to require care at all hours around-the-clock. This is not only exhausting for family, but they feel unprepared to handle the new and difficult needs of their loved one.

Consider even the simple aspect of getting out of bed so the sheets can be changed. With new extreme weakness it may take two people to get the person moved from the bed to a chair. Eventually as the person becomes even weaker it may be necessary to lift the person from the bed, or even make the bed with the person still in it, which is a skill in itself. It is no wonder that family members and other caregivers become exhausted. When a new healthcare problem arises everyone throws up their hands and sends their loved one to the hospital.

One would hope staff at the hospital will identify that the situation is dire and that your parent is near the end of her life. The hospital can then help the family start hospice enrollment. With the support of the hospice team the person might be able to return home for her final days. The support of the hospice team eases the burden of care through their services and care team.

Another reason people end up in the hospital at the end of life is when the family is concerned about getting to the hospital. Perhaps the hospital is some distance away or potential traffic congestion could cause a long trip. The family may be concerned that waiting longer will make it even more challenging to get to the hospital if it is needed. This could lead the family to decide on hospital care more easily.

Going to the hospital when there is no medical reason to be there can be a mistake. Medicare admission criteria have become tight. Going to the hospital, when there really isn't a medical situation that warrants being there, can result in being sent back home. If a family chooses the hospital in a time of panic, they may well be faced with finding a way to get their loved one back home.

The trauma of the trip to the hospital and care in the emergency department will likely have other consequences too. If your parent was weak and struggling before going to the hospital, her condition is likely to be worsened by the hospital trip, brief though it was.

Ethnic and cultural differences also impact care at the end of life. In some cases there are beliefs that prohibit dying at home. Also, access to care options, including home hospice care, are frequently made available and chosen more often by white members of our society. If you are Latino or African-American it is statistically more likely that your parent will end up in the hospital for her final days. This is likely a matter of both availability and awareness about the service.

Just about everyone in a hospital situation is affected by the authority of the lab coats and official operations according to rules we don't know and don't understand. Complicating this situation for minority groups has traditionally been their greater tendency to respond to the position of authority of the hospital and its doctors.

Studies have also shown that some minority groups tend to believe that more care is better. That the best care will include doing anything and everything possible, including cardiac resuscitation and ventilator use. This means minority group members are more likely than whites to spend their final days in an intensive care unit of a hospital.

As you can see it is essential for you to know what your parent wants before you make the commitment to medicalize her final days. Be prepared to accept that there may come a time when continued attempts to battle the inevitable are no longer showing love and respect for your loved one.

Life's final moments

Recently medical scientists have worked to understand what happens in the final moments of life. As we have discussed earlier, most older people today will die following a lingering period of decline.

This often means the final days and weeks are a very quiet time. It is typical for the person to spend most of the time sleeping. When awake they might be too drowsy to have a meaningful conversation. At this late stage you are not likely to know how they are feeling and what they are experiencing. Conversations will be short and fragmented with gaps of minutes or hours between responses. Resolve to have your conversations about your parent's care and wishes before this stage when it is too late.

It is common for people to lose appetite and later to stop eating all together. Interest in drinking will also decrease. Finding foods and beverages that still appeal is more important at this stage than worrying about maintaining a balanced diet.

As the human body begins to shut down, scientists believe that the last senses to be lost are hearing and touch. This argues for paying attention to the sounds around the person. Conversations should demonstrate her continued connection to family and friends and never assume that what is being said is not heard or understood. Keeping the room quiet may be appreciated by some, however if your parent enjoys music, or television, or the sound of pets scampering in play, there is no reason to isolate her. With the pull toward more sleep it is likely that familiar noises will be appreciated and will not prevent sleep.

Don't forget the importance of touch. Touch the loved one with fondness and consideration which means you must go beyond the merely functional touching of daily care routines. Touch that is familiar and caring can be very comforting.

Some people experience pain toward the end of life but with today's use of medications most pain can be diminished or even completely controlled. If your parent is receiving hospice care, the care team will balance medications for pain with your parent's wishes to participate in life around her. Too much pain medication can lead to grogginess. Let your parent guide her care so that she is able to balance management of pain and her ability to maintain a reasonable level of alertness.

As the end approaches the older person will likely just seem to fade away. She will even seem, and indeed will become, smaller.

It is worth repeating that near the end of life it is common to experience difficulty in swallowing and there may be coughing. You may have heard of the so-called "death rattle" and it may be disturbing when you hear it. It is cause by fluids – such as saliva and bronchial secretions – that accumulate in the throat and upper chest. Healthcare practitioners are confident that it does not mean the person is in pain. In my own professional experience I have never seen any indication to the contrary.

In the final fading away people lose consciousness. This can last for hours, sometimes even for days. It is believed that if there was pain previously it decreases during this period. It may seem like the person is dreaming. Perhaps they are.

They float in and out of consciousness. Sometimes they mutter things that seem meaningless. Maybe. On the other hand, the mutterings of a dying person might have meaning we can't understand.

The final few minutes are likely to be no different from the minutes before. Their slow and irregular breathing just stops at some point. No drama, no protracted, agonizing scenes of departure. They just peacefully stop breathing and their life is over.

They have moved on.

11
Know this and be in control

Even if your parents are in reasonably good health and their chronic conditions are stable, they will still have an occasional encounter with the healthcare system. They will have at least an annual medical appointment with a primary care physician and probably a few medical appointments with different specialty physicians.

Once you understand your parents' goals, preferences for life and care choices, the next step is to understand how best to advocate for their wishes during these medical encounters. This starts with understanding which doctors – and which specialists – are involved in their care and a bit about how it all fits together.

Your parent may be lucky and only have a few physicians that she sees, but as her medical condition becomes more complicated she will probably see several different physicians. She should have a primary care physician, probably either an internal medicine doctor or a family medicine doctor. She might also have a pulmonologist for her lungs, a cardiologist for her heart, a rheumatologist for her arthritis, a dermatologist for her skin, an ophthalmologist for her glaucoma, and so on. The number of doctors involved tends to increase with age and frailty.

While there are reasons for obtaining medical advice from specialists, seeing several physicians can also open the door to confusing and contradictory diagnoses, conflicting information, and contradictory recommendations. It can also lead to unnecessarily duplicated tests and procedures. Having a primary care physician helps reduce overlapping tests and procedures, but it may not eliminate them.

Fortunately, more and more physicians are using electronic health records. This keeps medical information on a central computer that is shared by many physicians as well as the hospital where they practice. Improved access to information reduces duplication and improves coordination between various medical services.

Medicare encourages the development of organized structures that bring physicians together with financial incentives to provide more efficient and effective care. Better information, communication and coordination help reduce duplication and lead to fewer treatment and medication errors, and better care outcomes.

If your parent does not have a primary care physician, now would be a good time to find one. Her primary care physician will communicate with the other physicians to keep informed about all of her conditions and medical treatments. This doctor is typically the only one with a complete picture about your parent's health and active medical treatments.

Not all physicians have special education in the care of older adults. Geriatricians are physicians who specialize in geriatric care – care of the elderly – and have had additional training and are board certified. Geriatricians are well attuned to identifying secondary problems that can result from chronic medical conditions. They look for side effects of medication interactions. They watch for things like dehydration, depression, skin break-down and other risk factors that come with advanced age. Geriatricians are most often affiliated with universities. Despite the growing number of older people in the population of the U.S., geriatricians are quite rare in most communities.

Most general internists and some family practice physicians care for large numbers of older patients. While they may not take the extra steps to become certified as geriatricians they often focus a portion of their continuing education on geriatric medicine.

Those physicians who care for the largest population of older adults in their practice are most likely to be open to learning what is best for your parent to improve his function and independence. You don't need to find a physician with a sub-specialty in geriatric care, but it is good to find physicians who have some specialized education in geriatrics. When your parent is looking for a new physician you can look up quite a bit of information online. You can find out where the physician completed medical school and any special qualifications like being board certified in an area of medicine. You can also find out if they have a special interest in the care of older adults.

Healthcare professionals complete years of education to prepare for their jobs, and most never stop learning. They are required and encouraged by their professional associations, by their colleagues, and by the hospitals where they are affiliated to continue their education. You can ask about continued education in geriatric medical care.

Medicare recognizes that involvement of several physician specialists can result in fragmented medical care.

As mentioned this can be cumbersome and confusing to patients and can lead to more expensive treatment plans. To counter this problem general internists and family practice doctors in many communities practice in what are called medical homes.[17] In order to qualify as a medical home, the member physicians have to meet extra Medicare standards. Once qualified, the physicians assume a more comprehensive responsibility to work with others who are providing care to their patients. This change is quite new and is already producing improvements in medical care for older adults.

Medical homes are designed to include a care team. In addition to the physician, these practices will have a nurse practitioner, nurses and technologists who work with the doctor to manage care for the patients in their practice. The standards the physician follows mandate care plans that take into account patients' values, needs, interests and abilities. If your parent's physician has this new qualification then you, the family caregiver, should be included as part of the care team.

Central to the concept of the medical home is the coordination of all care. Your parent should receive support to schedule every type of care needed from tests to specialty care. Medical homes are also expected to be accessible to patients. This may mean that the office has after-hours care so that non-emergency needs can be addressed without having to take your parent to a hospital emergency room.

The medical home practice might also have electronic access with email and internet services that allow patients, and those they authorize, to see results of tests and procedures and summaries of medical appointments.

Electronic access is a more efficient way for patients and their representatives to communicate with a medical practice. With electronic access you no longer have to sit on hold to speak with a front office person, who then needs to relay your question to the nurse, who will relay your question to the doctor for response. Most people who have electronic access to their healthcare team love it.

If you are even just moderately comfortable using an internet browser you will find these resources to be helpful and convenient. If this sounds good to you but your parent's physician does not offer electronic access, a nudge from you might motivate them to bring their office up to speed and adopt this change in their practice.

One of the changes developed to improve care for older adults comes from the understanding that taking care of a person with one or more chronic illnesses is not the same as taking care of a patient with an acute illness. The goal in the management of chronic illness is not to cure the illness, but to help the person manage the condition for optimal health and quality of life. To create a better approach to managing chronic illness a group of physicians developed what is called a chronic disease model of care. This model suggests factors that are important to ensure the best outcomes for people with chronic disease. One essential factor of this model is for patients to become empowered and prepared to participate in making decisions about their care.

Doctors are becoming more accepting of informed, activated patients and many understand that a change in the traditional doctor-patient relationship will result in better clinical outcomes. If your parent's doctor doesn't appreciate your strong role in the care of your parent, you might want to consider finding a doctor who will.

We have talked about the many decisions regarding care that will need to be made over time. Some of these choices may not be easy and may impact safety, function, pain level, mental abilities and other factors. The choices regarding these treatment decisions will need to consider not just what is medically possible, but also what course of treatment fits with your parent's goals and values. There are steps you can take to prepare yourself for the responsibilities of your role of caregiver.

First and foremost is to fully understand, from a layman's perspective, your parent's medical status. Being an informed patient or caregiver helps you to work with healthcare providers as a partner in planning and implementing care. You are not just doing what you have been told to do; you understand what to do and why you are doing it. When there is a new symptom you will have a better idea of whether it is something you need to watch, when you should respond in a planned manner to bring things back under control, or if you should seek urgent medical evaluation.

Health professionals frequently refer to this as "understanding red flags." Some hospitals have created special printouts to help patients with congestive heart failure, diabetes and other chronic medical conditions. Sometimes these use the red, green and yellow colors of a traffic light. By following the guidelines on these printouts, individuals and families know when a symptom is in the green zone and everything is good to go, when a symptom is in the yellow zone and a sign for caution, and when the symptom is in the red zone and a call to the doctor or a trip to the emergency department is needed.

By understanding your parent's conditions and his potential red flags you will know when to call your parent's physician and you will be able to more clearly explain your reason for calling. Even if you don't have a red flags chart, you can ask specifically, "What are the red flags we should watch out for – the things that are important and require action?" This is terminology that will be familiar to healthcare professionals.

Being armed with reliable information about various medical conditions will increase your confidence. You will better understand what your parent's physician tells you about her medical conditions. You will know which questions to ask before you enter the exam room. Then, after a medical appointment, you can go online to look up information to clarify anything you did not understand.

As part of every medical appointment your parent's doctor will summarize a plan for treatments and medications in the form of a doctor's order. Just like a doctor's order was important with a couple of the advance directive documents, this order provides instructions for care. A doctor's order is a necessary step for nurses, physical therapists, pharmacists and others to have the authority to act according to the plan.

Without this medical order, diagnostic procedures and treatments cannot legally take place and neither Medicare nor private insurance will pay for services rendered.

Successful management of your parent's illness is not just about following doctor's orders. It is about taking responsibility. This starts with taking the responsibility to ask questions and gather information so you can learn what you need to know to help your parent manage his health. It is also about supporting him to learn more about his illness. It is about advocating for the treatment protocols that will fit best with his needs, abilities and values. After all, you are not working together to manage his illness to please the doctor. You are doing it to help your parent function as well as possible for as long as possible.

Of course, some people would rather have a doctor tell them what to do next. Having a doctor tell them what to do, or not do, can actually be quite powerful. For example, people are much more likely to quit smoking, lose weight or start to exercise if a physician advises this change.

Consider the case of an older man who hated using his walker because it always seemed to be in the way. Then one day he fell and ended up in the hospital emergency room. The ER doctor scolded him about the risk of falling and the importance of using his walker. The doctor said something like, "I don't want to see you in here with a broken hip because you fell when walking without your walker." As a result the man started using his walker regularly, at least whenever he left his house. No one in his family could have influenced that behavior as well as the doctor did.

You can't count on a doctor to say the right things or lay out everything a person needs to do to stay healthy and safe. Medical researchers agree that being an informed patient or caregiver engaged in care leads to the best outcomes of care. When older adults work to learn more about their illness, or families ask informed questions, the outcome is almost always better.

Individuals vary in their readiness to hear new information and to learn how to become more actively responsible for their care. If you are busy with work and your own family you may discount the significance of a physician's recommendations following a new diagnosis of a disease affecting your parent.

Consider, just as an example, how you might respond if your parent is diagnosed with chronic obstructive pulmonary disease. You may have thought her symptoms were just a cold that will eventually clear up. You might find your mind wandering to something like pressing demands at work while trying to focus on a nurse's instructions about changes that need to be made in your parent's lifestyle, diet, and activities. In such a case you are probably not paying adequate attention. Or perhaps you just aren't ready to hear this difficult new medical information.

You might need a little time to absorb this news and then go back to learn what needs to happen to help your parent live more successfully with this new condition. Maybe you need to learn this information a piece at a time. If you are lucky, professional staff in your parent's doctor's office will pick up on your reticence and respond in ways that fit your readiness for information.

Medical professionals understand that providing education and information to help patients manage their chronic illness is important. But sometimes they go overboard when they prepare this information. A cardiac rehabilitation program I know of put together beautiful color folders packed with information. They included everything anyone could ever want to know about heart disease, treatments, medications, risks, diet, exercise, sleep suggestions and more. Plus full color brochures about the institution and all of its care programs.

Most patients and families accepted the beautifully printed folders with all the encyclopedic information.

They reported being pleased to get information that would answer their questions. They even seemed pleased that the treatment center cared enough to provide them with so much information.

Once they got home, however, I suspect the folder was set down on the hall table to be looked at later. "Later" became even later and soon the information packet was buried under incoming mail. There was just too much information so it was overwhelming. Someone at the treatment center might refer to it again, but usually not.

If you find yourself in a situation like this, divide the materials into manageable parts. Pull out just the pieces of information that provide guidance to support your parent's current health and care advice. Everything else can be set aside. You can review the other, usually more general information about your parent's condition and other services later if you need it.

There is another promising practice change slowly taking place in healthcare across the country. Healthcare professionals are becoming better prepared to support individual preferences. This is typically referred to as *person-centered care*. In many ways this approach to care is really an old approach.

Decades ago a general practice doctor would take care of an entire family, sometimes several generations of the family. He knew the history and development of an individual's illness as well as the amount of support the person had at home. With this knowledge he could guide the individual and his family in care.

Today, though, providing person-centered care is much more difficult. Healthcare delivery systems are designed for efficiency and clinical effectiveness. To be most responsive to individual differences, each person may require different information or a different approach to treatment. But this approach works. Even care for persons with dementia has benefited from a focus on the individual person's behavior, personality and values.

Healthcare providers who are trying to provide person-centered care will encourage patients to take more responsibility for their care and to actively participate in decisions about care. They will consider not just the current medical problem but how this problem is both affected by and effects other medical and social aspects of a person's life.

Become more informed

Learning about the medical conditions that affect your parents is easier today. You don't need specialized education or access to medical libraries. With access to the internet you have a wealth of information at your finger tips, at whatever hour of the day or night that you have time or need to look for information. If you are not already familiar with how to complete an internet search and how to decide which sources of information are worth reading, someone at your local senior center or public library can help you learn. You might also have a member of your family willing to introduce you to finding online health information.

With so many health-related websites available on the internet it is not difficult to find reliable information to help understand medical conditions. You can usually tell from the sponsor of a website and the author's credentials whether or not to trust the information. If the website is legitimately hosted by a major medical center or a nationally recognized, disease-related association, you can probably rely on the information. But caution is always required. Look at different websites to see if there is agreement about the information you find. And do not automatically believe or trust everything you find on the internet. If you are not reasonably knowledgeable about subjects like phishing [sic], identity theft, privacy and security, it is a good idea to search for materials on "internet safety" to learn how to protect yourself. You certainly do not have to become a security expert, but there are some areas and practices you should be aware of and follow.

You can find online discussions about many medical problems and various treatment options as well as medication benefits and side effects. If you are interested you can even find pictures of anatomy so you can see what part of the body is affected by an injury or condition.

Like I said, not everything on the internet is factual and true. Looking up treatment options on Wikipedia is not reliable, but the site can give you a start by providing topics you can search elsewhere for more reliable information. You probably do not need to be admonished not to try diagnosing an illness or condition yourself; "see your doctor first" is still good advice.

Many people have learned to value the internet as a source of health information. In fact, the top three sources of health information are doctors, family or friends, and the internet. People use the internet to prepare for a doctor's appointment or to look up additional information after a doctor's appointment.

You can also participate in chat discussions with others who have similar problems to give you confidence to ask the questions that concern you about your parent's health. Some chronic conditions have online support communities. If you find good peer sites they can be useful both in providing ideas as well as the support of knowing that there are others dealing with the same problems facing you.

Patients who do a little research on the internet often find themselves better able to ask informed questions. Anyone who is less fearful and less dependent has more confidence in their ability to evaluate and use the information provided by their doctor to make care decisions. Ultimately information helps to keep your parent in charge of care decisions. This isn't to discount your doctor's opinion, but if you and your parent understand her medical conditions better, you can become partners in care.

Family and friends are another frequently used source of health information. Talking with a relative who had a similar health condition can be invaluable. Listening to their detailed explanations and suggestions can be a great source of information. Again, though, caution is important. Aunt Susie's experience or Uncle Howard's advice might be helpful, but be prepared to take it a grain of salt. Check out anything you hear like this with qualified sources and your parent's doctor before making any changes.

Step up to the role of advocate

Serving as your parent's advocate and later as healthcare agent you will want to help her stay as engaged and healthy as possible. This will require you to interact with the healthcare delivery system in various ways.

If you don't know already, you will learn that the healthcare system, such as it is, doesn't always work the way you would like it to. Sometimes the right hand doesn't know what the left hand is doing, so to speak. Despite some systems' improvements in communication and coordination between care delivery sites and health professionals, some systems still don't get it. Changes are happening, but not very fast. It is still possible to get lost in some gap of care or information.

Even the best intentioned healthcare providers find it is hard to change decades of practice and culture. Historically, doctors made decisions and patients were expected to accept their advice and be compliant.

You may not know this but if you don't do what your doctor recommends, or writes as orders, you are considered *non-compliant.* There are many possible reasons a person might not be willing or able to follow through with a doctor's treatment plan. As examples a person might experience unpleasant side effects, or not be able to purchase the necessary supplies or equipment, or perhaps misunderstands the instructions. Many of these reasons have nothing to do with willful non-compliance. It is time for more patients to stand up and demand to be part of the care team. It is, after all, the person you care for and her family that this is all about.

Keep in mind that there is only one common variable as a person interacts with the healthcare delivery system to receive care: the person him- or herself. The following chapters will help a motivated individual, or family member on his behalf, to stay in charge of his own care and reduce the chances of error and duplication. It will not always be the easiest thing in the world to be an active and engaged caregiver and advocate for your parent. But you can do it. That way the care she gets will be more likely to match her goals and wishes.

Improving care for older adults

Improving care for older adults goes beyond the care provided by physicians. Other national changes through Medicare encourage attention to quality outcomes and better cooperation between the various types of care from hospitals to home-based care.

A consequence of these changes is shorter hospital stays. Shorter hospital stays mean that as a family member you may find you are thrust into responsibility much faster and deeper than you ever expected. When you get to chapter 15 you will find ways to help your parent after a hospital stay.

In addition to the guideline mentioned earlier, the American Geriatrics Society has made some important contributions to improve care provided by all physicians. They continue to develop care guidelines to assist those physicians who do not have specialty training in geriatrics.

The Society developed a medication list called the Beers List.[18] It provides guidance and precautions for use of medications with older adults to improve medication safety. This list includes medications that are potentially inappropriate for older adults, or that may increase potentially adverse side effects. As examples, medications like antidepressants and sleeping pills can lead to an increase in falls. Some other medications on the list increase risk for incontinence, mental changes, nausea, diarrhea or kidney malfunction. Because older adults' body systems handle medications in slightly different ways than younger people, some medications are less effective when used with older adults and some should be given in different doses.

Other guidelines help physicians consider medical tests and treatments that are supported by medical evidence in older patients. The focus of this is to reduce unnecessary testing and treatments. There are also care guidelines to improve the quality of care through better focus on the individual person's health status and goals. This benefits people with several medical problems.

When a new medication is prescribed you can ask if the medication is considered safe on the Beers List of medications. The same goes for recommendations for tests and treatments. You can ask if the recommended treatments are included on the list developed by the American Geriatrics Society on their Choosing Wisely list.[19] Who knows, maybe you will prompt your parent's physician to increase his or her continuing education focus to learn more about care of older adults.

Medical professionals have begun to speak up in favor of reducing unnecessary treatments. Their bias has been to "do more." Some label that an overuse of medical treatments. There are even groups of medical professionals working together to establish treatment guidelines that focus on the reduction of over-treatment.

To successfully reduce over-treatment will require the re-education of both physicians and patients. Physicians are following clinical guidelines when they recommend a course of treatment. Unfortunately, many of those guidelines were developed with middle-aged adults in mind, not patients in their 80s or 90s with multiple complicating health conditions. We can only hope that this is beginning to change.

Knowing and understanding the expected benefits and the potential risks for complications or long-term recovery will help you and your parent make the best treatment decisions for her.

Making decisions for care

When a physician you trust shares your parent's clinical test results with you and recommends a plan of treatment, the natural response is to accept the expertise of the physician and to agree to the recommended plan. But consider this: Physicians often opt for entirely different treatments when they are making decisions for themselves or their own family members. It does not hurt to push back against recommended treatment plans with in-depth questions and pointed queries. Insist on "slow" medicine and engage in your own due diligence preparation before making medical care decisions. (Take another look at chapter 6 if you need to refresh your memory on making these care decisions.)

Do not lose sight of the fact that most healthcare is low tech, low intensity. This is especially true when managing the care for older adults who have multiple chronic illnesses. Symptoms change slowly in most cases and responsible actions will often prevent deterioration and the need to go to the hospital.

Keep a record of changes in symptoms of each illness. Equally important are records of any changes in sleep, diet, exercise, attitude, mobility, and other daily activities and functional abilities. Helping your parent maintain her highest level of health and functioning means keeping aware of what is normal and responding when something changes. Keep yourself informed so you can find the right care, at the right time, from the best healthcare source. Control of these care choices is almost always in the hands of your parent and you as her caregiver and healthcare agent.

Notes

[17] The medical home is also known as a patient-centered medical home, or PCMH. They are a team-based system of health care delivery with a focus on continuous and comprehensive care for patients in a coordinated effort to get the best health outcomes.

[18] The Beers Criteria Medication List indicates medications that are potentially inappropriate for use with elderly patients. Older adults may have increased risk for adverse drug results because of changes in their body chemistry and a reduced capacity to process medications. Taking multiple medications can increase the chances of undesirable drug interactions.

[19] Choosing Wisely (www.choosingwisely.org) provides guidance so that physicians ask questions before decisions are made to rush to a new test, treatment, surgery or medication. One treatment area they have targeted is the use of unnecessary tests before surgery. Another is reducing the use of feeding tubes for patients with advanced Alzheimer's disease. The guidelines provide an alternative to "doing more." This helps doctors and patients balance risks and benefits.

12
How to be assertive at a doctor's appointment

PREPARATION FOR A MEDICAL APPOINTMENT begins with actually making the appointment. It is important to clearly and succinctly declare the reason for the appointment. That way the doctor's office will allot the appropriate amount of time according to the reason for the appointment. Appointment times allowed on physician schedules can vary from ten minutes for a medication check to as long as an hour for a complete physical examination.

Your parent's doctor might want to spend more time with her during an appointment but be unable to. Standards have been established by Medicare and other insurance plans for the length of treatment times. Clinics also set standards for the number of patients each doctor sees in a day. Physicians are expected to meet these standards.

Let the office know if the visit is a routine annual visit or prompted by a special medical situation or change in condition. It is frustrating to discover when you get to the clinic that the appointment is just for a short medication check appointment when what you wanted was an annual Medicare Wellness Visit.[20]

Unless guided in another direction, scheduling staff will look at time availability and suggest an appointment time that might be a long time in the future. That could be okay when there is nothing unusual going on. But if your parent's condition has changed or there is some other pressing reason for a more timely appointment, tell the scheduler when you are making the appointment. If there is a health concern you can ask to speak to the nurse who works with your parent's doctor. By discussing the problem or concern with the nurse you may get her to request an earlier appointment.

Prepare for a doctor's appointment

Have you ever come out of a doctor's appointment, started to drive away and then given yourself a forehead slap because you forgot a question you meant to ask? Preparation will ensure this doesn't happen with your parent's appointment. Since the actual time your parent will have with the doctor will be short, go into the exam room prepared to get the information you need from the visit.

We all occasionally experience what is commonly called *white coat syndrome*. That is, we get a little anxious in a doctor's office. Blood pressure and pulse rate can rise and the brain doesn't seem to work as well. One thing that will help your parent is for you, or someone she trusts, to go with her. This person can be her second eyes and ears, as well as her advocate when needed.

Typically today the physician comes into the exam room and looks at a computer screen to take a look at test results, previous notes, or anything new since the

Chapter 12. How to be assertive...

last medical appointment. Some physicians are good at keeping a connection with patients while they review any new information. Unfortunately others are not and patients may feel they are less important than the computer screen.

Again and again it has been found that physicians aren't very good listeners. They are in a hurry and will cut off comments by patients, sometimes in seconds. If your parent is not prepared or is a bit anxious she may use these precious seconds or minutes to chat about things that aren't very important. Many people fail to realize the significant difference between a professional and a personal relationship. Healthcare relationships are strictly professional and personal chatter about subjects unrelated to the topic at hand are often unwelcome.

You can avoid irrelevant chatter with advance preparation and even rehearsal if you find that helpful. Rehearsal is particularly helpful if your parent has trouble talking about her medical problem. Or if she has trouble saying the words due to difficulties with pronunciation. Embarrassment can also be a stumbling block.

If for example your parent has a hard time getting to the bathroom in time and she finds this difficult to share, it can help for her to practice saying the relevant words. This should be done as directly and clearly as possible using facts when you can gather them.

Sometimes a little role playing helps. Pretend to be your parent's doctor and let her practice sharing the things that concern her. Encourage her to put into words how she has been feeling lately. *Do not interrupt her when she is doing this.* It does not help to speak a word or finish a sentence when she is having difficulty. Be patient. Once she has practiced expressing previously uncomfortable things it will be easier for her to say them to the doctor.

A visit to the doctor's office can be an outing that will perk your parent up, even if she has been tired or depressed. The visit puts her at the center of attention and when the doctor asks how she is doing she might just forget she has been tired or down in the dumps. If she has practiced stating how she has been feeling, that will help her remember the things she wants to share with her doctor.

In addition to rehearsal it helps to gather facts about your parent's changing condition. Keep a record of times when she has trouble breathing, or needs to rush to the bathroom, or when she forgets things. This is the kind of information that will help the physician develop a care plan.

Your parent may be comfortable taking the lead in preparing for her medical appointment. If not you may want to coach her along to be sure she stays focused on the things you both want from the appointment.

In his book *Being Mortal*, Atul Gawande, MD[21] suggests a few simple questions that doctors should ask their patients. By flipping these questions around here are some recommendations to help you and your parent prepare the information to share during your parent's medical appointment.

- *What is your understanding of your health or condition?* Review what you and your parent want to tell your parent's doctor about her health condition.

- *What are your goals if your health worsens?* Review your parent's goals so they can be shared. Also, make sure the doctor has a copy of her advance directive documents.

- *What are your fears?* You should encourage your parent to express any fears she has regarding various treatment options and about how the course of the illness will progress. Include her concerns or fears about the costs that she will have to pay for treatment.

- *What are the trade-offs you're willing to accept?* Review your parent's understanding about the benefits and burdens of various treatment options.

Make notes of the questions and information your parent wants to share with her doctor. That way you won't forget the important issues, even if you are nervous in the exam room.

If you and your parent have done your homework and prepared for the doctor's appointment you will be better prepared to get the most out of the appointment.

On the day of the appointment

What do you take to a medical appointment? At a minimum there are three lists you should take with you.

1. Medication list.

You should always take an up to date list of medications your parent currently takes. This list should include anything she takes whether prescribed or over-the-counter medications that she selected. That means including vitamins and herbal or natural remedies as well. You might not think these other things are important because they weren't prescribed by a physician, but some of them can interact with prescribed medications.

This list is particularly important if there have been any changes in medications since the last appointment. Your parent may see several doctors and each should have a complete picture of the medications your parent takes. (See a sample medication list in the appendix.)

Hopefully the physician's office uses electronic medical records and already has a list of medications on file in their system. But don't rely on the record being up-to-date. Bring a list of everything your parent currently takes.

2. Parent's condition list.

Take a list of all the salient facts that relate to your parent's condition. This might include changes in weight, eating patterns, sleep patterns, state of mind or other things you or she have noted.

3. Questions list.

Take a list of questions you want to ask and anything else you want to discuss with your parent's doctor. This should be a prompt-list for the things you and your parent want to learn from this medical appointment.

During the appointment the physician needs to assess the reason for the appointment and hear what your parent wants to express regarding her concerns. Your goal is to get maximum benefit from the appointment. Your preparation for the visit is essential so you can move quickly to the reasons for the visit and make the brief time worthwhile.

Physicians are not always easy to talk with. They tend to talk in their own language using words and phrases that you may not understand. Typically they will talk more to you than to your parent. You may need to remind them to talk to your parent. Also physicians are likely to interrupt your parent and you in their attempt to move things along.

Chapter 12. How to be assertive...

They are always aware of the patients who are waiting in other exam rooms and the schedule that needs to be kept. You may need to make clear your expectations for focused attention during the appointment.

It takes discipline to remember to talk about those things that are important for the physician to know to better plan and recommend the best course of action or treatment plan. The physician's focus will be on the one problem that brought you in to his office – so you may need to remind him that this problem fits into a complex context of multiple conditions and your parent's home situation.

Some years ago a program was developed to help parents and their children during medical appointments. Called *Ask Me 3* the program was designed to help children and parents become more aware of the things that affect health and to learn to take responsibility for their health.[22]

Ask Me 3 is designed around three questions. The questions are clear and easy to understand and remember. They are easily adapted for use with adults. These simple questions have been demonstrated to improve medical outcomes because they improve communication between patients and their healthcare providers. Practice them so you are prepared to ask them during the appointment.

- *What problem caused me to be at the doctor's office today?* Your parent or you need to be able to explain why you requested this doctor's appointment. Then you need to ask questions during the visit so you understand what the doctor learns through the examination.

- *What can I do to be better?* Ask if there are treatments, medications or perhaps other actions that will help with recovery. Again, make sure you understand the instructions.

- *Why do I need to do anything?* Sometimes doing nothing is okay, but sometimes doing nothing can have negative consequences. Ask enough questions to understand the treatment recommended and what could happen if you decide not to follow the recommendations.

If you keep these three questions in mind, you will be more likely to get the answers you seek and remember them. You will be better prepared to be more responsible for managing your parent's health.

When you consider your questions and things you want to share, jump right in early in the exam. Ask the most important question first. People often hesitate, especially with something causing them worry and concern. Then when the doctor has his or her hand on the door to leave the exam room your parent says, "just one more thing" adding something very important.

One of the likely things to happen at this point is that the doctor will say you will need to set up another appointment to review this new problem. So this leads to all the logistical problems of arranging for a new appointment and the anxiety of waiting longer for answers to your parent's question and concerns.

When your parent's doctor provides information about a new medical problem and recommendations for treatment you have both the right and responsibility to ask clarifying questions before care decisions are made. Ask about the benefits of the recommended treatment plan so you know what good things you can expect will happen if you proceed. But, also ask what risks are possible with the treatment.

Can your parent expect pain or functional losses? How long will recovery take? Are there other options for treatment? Go back to the discussion about slow medicine. Is the option recommended by the physician a slow medicine care choice. In some cases you can try a less intensive solution first and move on to another course of treatment if it doesn't work out. Your parent may be given just one course of treatment but remember that there are always others – including doing nothing. Have the courage to ask what else could be done.

In many situations when considering care options for older adults, especially frail older adults, the protocol calls for starting with simple things first. This is a considerate approach that balances the desire to fix the problem as quickly as possible while minimizing the risk of a negative consequence. It is also important that the treatment recommended is reasonable and doable.

For better or worse, the medical culture of the United States is biased toward prescribing medications. Many medications are life changing in helping people manage their chronic illness, but there are other reasons that prompt more prescriptions. Patients themselves can be a major problem. They see lots of medication ads and come to expect a medication for every problem that ails them.

When your parent is prescribed a new medication, this is definitely a time for questions. Before accepting a new medication the first question is whether there are non-medication approaches that would be effective. Then, you and your parent should be clear about what the medication is, why it is being prescribed, how long she should take it, and how and when she should take it. Ask about side effects and when a side effect might be serious. Sometimes side effects occur because a medication interacts with another one she already takes. So be sure to ask if there might be interactions with other medications. You can also ask the pharmacist these questions when you pick up the medication. Ask both the physician and the pharmacist – it never hurts to hear important information twice.

Some medications have special requirements such as taking with food, before a meal, or not with fruit juice. Some medications will require periodic blood tests to make sure the drug is doing its job and to make sure certain side effects aren't happening.

You and your parent need to understand what to expect when the proposed treatment is completed. Will she be able to return to the level of function she had before the medical problem prompted treatment? You want her to be prepared if there are risks of pain, skin breakdown, loss of appetite, or anything other potential side effect.

Unfortunately medical treatment recommendations can be made based on age and the doctor's perceptions about age. A doctor looks at an 80 year old man sitting on the exam table and thinks of the patient primarily as an old man. If the man complains about pain in his leg the doctor might well consider that normal because, hey, this is an old man. But what if this man has recently been mountain climbing and plans to scale another peak or two in coming months. To counter possible assumptions, he needs to tell the physician about related circumstances like this.

The doctor may believe that everyone of a certain age has aches and pains, or is forgetful, or is unable to process complicated information to make a decision. A doctor with this kind of narrow perspective is more likely to misdiagnose – or just plain miss – lots of conditions in older people. For example, mental depression in older adults is one of the most commonly unrecognized problems by physicians. If you rehearsed before the appointment your parent will have the words to express his individual situation and, if necessary, cut through the fog of the physician's presuppositions.

Make notes throughout the medical appointment. Record the problems that are identified as well as all options for treatment. Even if your parent and doctor make a decision easily, it is reasonable to assume that you or your parent will want to revisit the information discussed later, when you are no longer at the doctor's office.

Don't be passive. The clinical outcome will be better if you and your parent are engaged in her medical care.

If you are not able to join your parent for a doctor's appointment, suggest that she take a friend. To ensure that the maximum value is gained from the medical appointment, your parent should not go alone. Two people listening to a conversation is better than one – at any age. As a person gets older it is harder to absorb lots of new information quickly.

If your parent's knowledge of medical terminology is limited, has hearing or vision limitations, or has any cognitive decline, it is especially important that a second pair of ears be there during the medical appointment.

Even young, healthy people come away from medical appointments not sure what the doctor told them about the lump they are concerned about or the pain in their knee. It is hard to think, hard to hear everything that is said, and hard to remember what transpired during a medical appointment. Follow-up questioning has shown that none of us do a very good job of retaining information we hear during a doctor's appointment. We don't remember about half of what we have been told and even then what we think we were told is frequently wrong. Taking notes and having another person present can help make the most out of the visit.

At times your parent's primary care physician will want the opinion of a specialist to manage one of her medical conditions. Be sure you know why your parent is seeing this specialist just in case the information is not transmitted clearly. You don't want to show up for a specialist medical visit and learn that the specialist doesn't know why you're there. This can also be a problem with diagnostic tests. You take your parent for an MRI and the specific question to be addressed in the test is not clear in the result. The test doesn't provide the information the physician was seeking. So the physician has to send your parent back for a second test.

This need to keep track of care recommendations, tests and treatments becomes more complicated as additional physicians are added to the care team. Chapter 16 will provide more specific ideas for how to set up a system to track and manage your parent's care.

Keep in mind that physicians have different levels of expertise and experience. You can seek a second opinion and no one will think any the worse of you for asking for one. In choosing another professional for the second opinion you can ask about credentials, including special certifications. You can find out if complaints have been filed or if there is any history of disciplinary action.

If your parent needs a specialist or a surgeon, you want someone who has the expertise and experience to provide the best care and treatment. You can ask how often the doctor has treated the medical problem or performed the specific surgery.

Be wary about accepting the recommendations of friends or relatives. Remember that even the wackiest of quacks have at least a few supporters who think they are just great. Don't even accept recommendations from your parent's primary physician without asking at least a few questions.

We hear what we want to hear

When someone we care about is struggling with a medical problem and not feeling very well, or unable to think clearly on their own, we just want them to be better. We want them to be back to the fully functioning, engaged person they were before this illness.

When we ask questions of doctors and nurses we have our ears set to hear good news. No one likes to hear or deliver bad news. In a physician's attempt to deliver bad news gently families often only hear the good parts of the message.

The new information can be overwhelming and what the older person and family might hear is blurred and mixed up. Confusion and miscommunication are very common. Problems can result from misunderstanding information about the illness, its seriousness and the options for treatment. The resulting understanding is worse, especially when the news is not good.

It is not unusual for individuals and family members to come away from such conversations wondering what was said. They may even be convinced that they heard something entirely different from the intended message. If several people were listening each is likely to hear something different.

Sometimes family members disagree with the physician's assessment of the situation. This misunderstanding can go both ways with some thinking the situation is worse than they are told. Most of those who misunderstand the message, though, tend to have a rosier view of what was said.

This kind of selective hearing that leans more toward optimism seems to be progressively more pronounced as loved ones near the end of life. Family members and friends want to present a sense of optimism for the person who is dying so the person will keep fighting to live. However, some older people don't want that; they feel they have had a good life and it is time to go. They may be frustrated with a slow decline, loss of function, or dealing with uncomfortable treatments. But they may agree to continued treatment just because their family members want them to.

It is almost always difficult to hear bad news about your parent's health. You can expect to feel conflicted when you do. The best antidote to this conflicted emotion is a full understanding of what your parent wants. Knowing that will help you work through the conflict.

If you know she wants to keep fighting and have every test and treatment possible to live as long as possible, your decision to proceed when a doctor lays out a course of possible action will be easier. Likewise, if you know her goal is to die quietly at home, with family nearby, your decision about care options is easier.

A physician can give you an idea about what will come next for your parent but you won't find anyone who will confidently tell you what to expect with various treatment options. What will come next, how long it will take to recover, how long your parent will have the ability to function on her own or with support, how long this next phase will continue before another change in condition, and other questions are all hard to predict. Physicians who are experienced in the care of older adults can provide some guidance but it is unwise for them to make promises about the future.

Notes

[20] A Medicare Wellness Visit will review your health and update your personal prevention plan. Medications are reviewed. Routine measures are taken including height, weight, and blood pressure. Periodic screening for memory loss, depression and falls risk are included.

[21] Being Mortal: Medicine and What Matters in the End by Atul Gwande, Metropolitan Books, 2014, www.atulgawande.com

[22] *Ask Me 3*. National Patient Safety Foundation bit.ly/2HHqbFm

13
Hospitalization happens!

As discussed earlier, chronic illness lasts for years, often decades. As time goes on it would be unusual for your parent to not require hospitalization at some point.

The expansion of outpatient services makes the hospital a pretty diverse place. Many procedures and surgeries take place without the need for inpatient hospital care. Many trips to the hospital facilities may be for diagnostic procedures, or a wide range of outpatient treatments.

Sometimes the treatment of urgent or more serious medical problems requires admission for an inpatient stay at the hospital. You may have time to discuss the options for care with your parent and her physician before selecting hospitalization and the proposed treatment there. On the other hand, crises can happen that result in urgent trips to a hospital emergency room. There was not time to debate pros, cons, benefits or burdens – your parent is at the hospital and new decisions need to be made.

The role of hospitals in care has changed. Days spent in a hospital bed are just a small episode in the total course of managing most illness for older adults. That said, many hospitals still tend to think they are the center of healthcare. Their clinical staff move ahead with treatment plans without much regard for the care and support being provided in the community by family and other community services.

Many hospitals are part of a large healthcare organization with branch locations throughout the community. These can include diagnostic and treatment centers for particular medical problems as well as urgent care centers and physician practice settings. They might also include a home health agency, a medical equipment supplier, and other services. Some large healthcare organizations even include senior housing, assisted living, nursing home and hospice care.

Even the best of these healthcare organizations can have hospital staff who know very little about care outside of the hospital. They might have no idea about what happens with home and community-based care and only a superficial knowledge of how people manage life with chronic illness on a day-to-day basis in their homes.

It is usual for the number of hospitalizations to increase in the last years of life. The frequency of hospital admission has declined thanks to the advent of more outpatient- and home-based care. Not only have the number of hospital admissions gone done, there has also been a reduction in the average number of days patients remain there once they are admitted. These earlier releases after shorter stays often leave families feeling like the patient was discharged too soon.

Tighter Medicare and health plan admission rules restrict hospital admission to only those cases that cannot be managed in another setting. Patients in the emergency department are evaluated to determine if their circumstances and condition qualify them for inpatient admission at the hospital. Many patients and their families are shocked when they learn that they do not qualify for hospital admission. But your parent could be in the hospital overnight, maybe even moved to a bed that is not in the emergency room. Under certain circumstances this can happen and she will still technically be an outpatient.

Your parent might be in what is called *observation status*. Patients are supposed to be informed if they are in observation care but this does not always happen. Time spent in an observation bed is considered outpatient care. You probably know that hospital costs for inpatient care are covered under Medicare Part A (after an annual deductible). But observation status is different.

As of this writing it is possible for patients to be classified as under observation care for up to 48 hours. Like any other outpatient service, Medicare Part B covers this care. The reimbursement rate however is different and lower. People who receive Medicare Part B benefits are responsible for 20 percent of the cost for each outpatient service received. Depending on the services received and the amount of time spent in observation care this can add up. In addition there are some services that will not be covered by Medicare Part B during observation, including medications.

This has a couple of significant consequences. First, the bill for the hospital care might be unexpected and significant. Other coverage may help. Medigap policies will cover the deductible and copays and Medicare Part D prescription drug plans may cover the costs of any medications. Second, without qualifying days spent in the hospital, Medicare will not cover post-hospital care for rehabilitation at a nursing facility or in home health care.

Any time your parent is in the hospital for a night or more you will want to find out if she was in an *observation bed* or an *inpatient bed* before considering options for post hospital care.

When you or an ambulance take your parent to a hospital emergency room a hospital staff person will complete what is called *triage* to determine how sick your parent appears to be. The triage process prioritizes the patients who are waiting for care to determine who can wait to be seen, and who needs to be seen by doctors more quickly.

Most patients will wait in the emergency department, sometimes for quite a long time, because the patient's medical problem is not considered life-threatening. Patients who are considered to be experiencing an emergency, potentially life-threatening status will have priority.

Most older patients arrive at the emergency room either because of new symptoms related to a chronic illness or because of an injury such as a fall. Many of these patients will be considered less urgent. This can result in long waits in the hospital emergency department.

When a person is considered to be in a life-threatening emergency situation the emergency department shifts into high gear. Everything that can be done to save the life will be done, unless you make a strong effort to stop the process. Remember the idea of the slippery slide for medical care.

As you might expect, emergency room doctors do not have time for conversations. You will need to know what your parent would have wanted in this potential situation in order to act quickly to state approval or disapproval for requests to perform various tests and procedures.

Even if your parent is able to make decisions for herself, the speed and stress of the situation may lead to decisions that she would not make in any other circumstance. A family member, or friend, can advocate for her wishes if present at the hospital when decisions are being made.

If your parent has cognitive problems – even mild ones – the need for vigilant advocacy increases. Your parent may still be articulate and sound confident. The healthcare staff may make assumptions that she is able to make her own medical decisions.

In some cases this can lead to care that is dangerous. Information has to be accurate. Questions such as: Can you stand? Do you need help? Are you a diabetic? Do you have any metal in your body? must be answered correctly. Wrong answers can lead to serious problems with certain diagnostic procedures.

Your parent may give permission for procedures, tests or even surgery without understanding what she has agreed to. The person who is her healthcare agent should be prepared to step in when decisions are being made. If you are her agent but don't speak up, or if you do not have the legal evidence to show you are her healthcare agent, decisions can be made without you, despite your protestations.

Even though medical personnel in emergency rooms treat a large number of older patients, their training is focused on life saving treatments. Most do not know how to identify cognitive decline in a patient until it becomes significant and obvious. And few emergency room (ER) personnel have had training in the special needs of older patients.

When your parent goes to the hospital you will need to take not just her identification and insurance cards but other information about your parent's health and condition. In a later chapter you will receive guidance to put together a Go Folder. This will be covered in more detail later, but the basics you should be prepared take are:

- a list of medical problems;

- a list of medications;

- information on any disabilities such as hearing and vision loss that can impact communication or treatment decisions; and

- copies of her advance directive documents.

Taking this information to the hospital can help prevent mistakes and misunderstanding. This information should be kept where either you or your parent can grab the critical information before heading out the door. It is also a good idea for you, as caregiver, to keep copies of these items to reference in the event of an emergency.

The situation of being in the emergency department is overwhelming for anyone. The sounds, lights, smells, noise and unfamiliarity of the situation, added to the reason your parent is there in the first place, can make it hard to understand what is being said to her. Making decisions can be very difficult. Having a family member present can help manage the stressful situation and prevent misunderstandings.

Consider a woman in her nineties who was taken to the hospital emergency department after a fall. She was exasperated with herself for losing her balance, and since it was the middle of the night she was also quite tired. She worried about whether her leg was broken and whether this meant she would have to spend time away from her home and miss the spring flowers. Or worse, whether she would even be able to return home at all.

When she was asked routine questions to determine her ability to make her own medical decisions, she found them insulting and irrelevant. For example: What day is it? Where are we? The staff person named three objects and asked her to repeat them. She considered the questions to be silly so she gave silly answers. She failed the mini-mental exam. She was labeled with cognitive loss and possible dementia. Later, in a rehabilitation center, the staff was surprised to find she was very alert, oriented and intelligent. They repeated the test with very different results.

Your parent will need to be able to process new information in the strangeness of the hospital setting. She wants her medical problem to be resolved so she can go home. If someone suggests a solution, she may be eager to agree. Add to that the tendency of some to become passive in these situations and agree with anyone in a position of authority. Even if your parent is able to make her own decisions she will benefit by having someone with her to advocate for her preferences.

While your parent is in the hospital she will be cared for by a number of people from numerous departments. Electronic medical records make it easier for staff in one area to keep staff in other departments informed. But problems can still occur if complete information isn't passed along.

Your parent may or may not be able to answer questions and remember the critical information that needs to be shared with staff. Throughout your parent's inpatient stay family and close friends should be readily available to advocate for her needs and wishes as well as to protect her from harm.

During your parent's illness and hospitalization keep track of the steps of treatment, the diagnostic tests and procedures that were conducted, and the information you are given. You might find a notebook or a file on your phone or computer is a way to store this information. During the stay or later you and your parent might need to refer back to the events and the new information gained during the hospital stay.

If your parent is somewhat uncertain or confused about her stay in the hospital, reviewing your notes will help. This record will help to clearly explain what happened and what she can expect when she is home again.

Since the hospital stay was likely a disorienting and stressful time you may need to repeat this information several times. The notes you kept about her stay will help you give her the same information each time she asks.

Be alert to hazards of hospital care for older adults

Older patients are less resilient. They are physically and mentally less able to cope with unusual and stressful situations.

Hospital treatment can be effective in managing an acute illness. However, the patient will almost always be weaker and less able to do the things they were able to do before being hospitalized.

It is not unusual for hospitalization for one problem to result in other problems. A recent study found that one in three patients over 70 (and half of the patients over 85) were *more* disabled after being hospitalized. This was true even if they recovered from the original cause of their hospital stay. Because of this, more home care and support are needed following hospitalization. Older adults will likely need help with more daily living activities like dressing, walking and bathing. Remember the concept of the dwindles. The hospitalization is a blip along the likely path of occasional illness and decline that most people will face in the last years of life.

While your parent is in the hospital you will find that the staff will be focused on resolving the problem that caused the admission, such as complications of a heart condition. They may not pay as much attention to making sure your parent is getting enough to eat and drink. They also are not likely to be sure your parent gets out of bed regularly (as soon as it is safe).

The treatments in the hospital may include such things as monitors, oxygen tubing and intravenous treatment poles, all of which make it more difficult to get up or move around. And noise and monitoring make it difficult to sleep at night.

For older patients these conditions are more than annoying. The older and more frail a person is, the more serious the potential for complications caused by hospitalization. Just the prolonged stay in bed itself is damaging with muscle loss every day.

In 2010 the U.S. Department of Health and Human Services (DHHS)[23] reported that more than one in four hospitalized Medicare patients experience harm as the result of their hospital care.

Half of these patients experienced harm with serious consequences, including death. The other half of the one-in-four who experienced harm had less serious, temporary consequences. In their analysis the DHHS concluded that almost half of the harmful, unintended consequences to hospital patients could have been prevented. It is these unintended consequences – the harmful, preventable events – that require your vigilance and advocacy to help protect your parent.

This is not to say that older people should not go the hospital when more intense care is needed, or when an acute health crisis occurs.

Please understand my purpose here, which is to inform you of the need for caution and to remain alert to some commonly occurring problems related to hospitals and being treated in them. I have never heard of a hospital that was overtly uncaring or trying to do harm. In my experience, both as a healthcare practitioner and as an administration executive, hospitals are staffed by people who care and want to do their best for patients. And hospitals are getting better at this every day; many are exemplary. So do not be afraid to use a hospital when that is called for. On the other hand, if hospitalization is not necessary in a given circumstance, ask if another mode of treatment is possible to avoid potential problems of hospitalization.

Hospitals have to keep track of a tremendous amount of data for quality review and billing purposes. Their payment from Medicare and health plans can be impacted by such things as incidence of falls or infections. They can be financially penalized for hospital re-admissions that occur within 30 days of discharge. But hospitals are not evaluated or paid based on many of the potential negative consequences of hospital care for older adults.

Chapter 13. Hospitalization happens!

Enforced immobility is part of the reason for many of the problems that can occur as a result of hospitalization. The next chapter will explain these in more detail, but here are some of the more common hazards of hospitalization:

- Loss of muscle strength and functional ability.
- A slip or fall.
- Delirium, confusion or dementia.
- Skin breakdown and pressure sores.
- Urgency, frequency and loss of bladder control.
- Pills, pills and more pills.
- Medical errors.
- Malnutrition and dehydration.
- Feelings of loss, isolation and depression.
- Unwanted or inappropriate treatment.

Some hospitals have protocols in place to counteract the negative impact of the hospital stay. As a family member, you can encourage these interventions. Use any such tools available to you, and your own preparedness, to be a better advocate to protect your parent from the potential negative consequences from time spent in the hospital.

Start when you enter the hospital. Share your parent's goals and concerns and advocate for their wishes when the plan of care is developed. Every hospital will say that they develop care plans with patients and with their goals guiding care, but in practice this is not consistent. Having the physician, or even a care team, prepare a plan of care and then reviewing it with your parent, and hopefully with you, is not developing the plan of care with your parent.

Her concerns and goals need to be known at the start of the care plan. This has to become a mantra for any caregiver: *What does SHE want?* The plan should present the best medical or clinical course of action. And the best course of action consistent with your parent's goals for her life as well as to minimize the potential hazards of hospitalization.

Fortunately more hospitals now include a focus on returning to self-care and preparing for returning to home. The next chapter will review briefly each of the potential risks of hospitalization and provide some suggestions for families so you can be alert and prepared to advocate for your parent's best interest.

You may initially feel a sense of relief when your parent is in the hospital. A whole staff of responsible people are looking after her and taking care of her. But an understanding of the potential hazards of a hospital stay will prepare you to anticipate risks before there are serious consequences. Much as you may feel the need for one, this is not a time for you to take a break.

Notes

[23]Levinson, Daniel, Adverse Events in Hospitals: National Incidence Among Medicare Beneficiaries. Office of the Inspector General, Department of Health and Human Services, November 2010.

14
Ten common hazards of hospitalization and what to do about them

WHEN YOUR PARENT is in the hospital your role as family caregiver shifts a bit. You can turn over the day-to-day care of your parent to hospital staff who are trained and prepared to manage your parent's illness or injury. You can be confident of their clinical skills and the compassionate care they provide to your parent.

In almost all circumstances hospitals are safe places and the best place to be for treatment and care of serious illness. The problem is that your parent is at an advanced age. The hospital staff will focus on the management of the illness or injury that prompted the admission. They may miss some potential hazards that can cause unintended consequences to impact the health and well-being of a vulnerable, frail older patient.

This chapter covers ten of the most common hazards that require vigilance on your part during your parent's hospital stay. If you understand the main issues and are observant, you can be confident that you have done what could be done to protect your parent from possible harm while she is recovering from the problem that brought her to the hospital.

Loss of muscle strength and functional ability

When I started my work in healthcare I was an occupational therapist. I worked in a rehabilitation setting focused on post-hospital care for Medicare patients. Coming from the perspective of rehabilitation my frame of reference for care has at its core the importance of activity and exercise. And the hazards of lying in a bed.

I never saw anyone discharged from the hospital with the same strength and endurance they had before they were hospitalized. Of course this seems obvious, the individuals were still recovering. But the seriousness of the consequences of loss in strength and physical ability are often not considered in hospital or post-hospital care. The potential loss of muscle and diminished functional ability increases tremendously with age. Sarcopenia – the natural loss of muscle with aging – is a problem anyway. Enforced inactivity of a hospital stay causes significant muscle loss. Researchers in one study found that healthy people in their 70s confined to bed for 10 days could lose 10 percent of their leg muscle mass. As patients become older the negative impact of bed rest increases.

As a rule it takes about two weeks of conditioning exercise for an older person to recover from every day spent in bed. Think about how you feel after you have been ill for even a short time. When you get up again you are wobbly and unsteady on your feet. Now add a few years and the impact is even more significant. It is normal to lose muscle as we get older (sarcopenia) but adding bed rest accelerates the process of muscle loss. In fact the list of negative complications from inactivity

Chapter 14. Ten common hazards of hospitalization...

reads like a medical disaster: cardiac and cardiovascular complications; disuse osteoporosis; skin, gastrointestinal, metabolic, nutritional and urinary changes; and on and on. These are just a few of the multitude of what are called "adverse clinical manifestations" of bed rest. For some it may not be possible to recover completely from the prolonged inactivity of a hospital stay.

Even if one can avoid hospitalization we know that many older adults gradually become less active as they age. This seems normal. There are fewer demands for physical activity and a downward spiral of inactivity begins. Each time we cut out an activity – like going to work, mowing the grass, doing the laundry – we lose a little of the ability to do these activities.

People who maintained a hectic pace of life with long work days are surprised to discover later, after they have retired, that an afternoon of moderate activity wears them out. The well known phrase "use it or lose it" definitely applies. Reduced activity has consequences. Like loss of strength, balance and functional ability. Some of the various aches, pains, stiffness and other insults of aging experienced by older people might be alleviated by something as simple as being more active.

Unsurprisingly it is difficult to get older adults to accept this. Patients recovering from surgery or illness are more likely to be convinced that rest is what they need to recover. Caring family members will say, "just rest" or "take it easy now" when they should suggest she walk around the halls or maybe "you'll feel better if you sit up in the chair for a while."

Muscle strength is critical for maintaining balance and the ability to walk safely. At some point muscle loss is so significant that complete recovery is no longer possible, even with hard work.

As muscle strength declines so does functional ability. Most significant is the ability to walk. In a normal day your parent probably does not need to walk much. This relative lack of exercise costs her in other areas. Like the ability to get out of bed safely, get dressed, or just walk normally around the house. Consider, for example, the consequences to your parent and to you if she can no longer get up at night and walk safely to the bathroom, or even manage a bedside commode. This can be a game changer.

Remember the home safety discussion in chapter 5. Your parent doesn't have to be in a hospital to experience muscle loss. Anytime she reduces her activity she will experience muscle loss. This process is a downward spiral in which each episode of illness leads to a further loss of strength and function.

The progression of debility in the elderly is predictable. After one illness your parent might stop going to the grocery store. She no longer takes walks around the block. After awhile she finds it difficult to walk to the car. It gets harder and harder for her to get out of a chair so she spends more time just sitting. The gradual decrease in movement and activity is a slippery slope that makes it easy to lose muscle strength and much harder to build it back up again.

The loss of muscles and strength has a significant negative impact on the ability to continue living at home and remain independent. This is particularly true when the muscle strength in the legs is lost. Strength in the leg muscles is essential to be able to stand and walk. The natural tendency of the elderly to avoid unnecessary movement is abetted by what seems like a conspiracy to "make life easier." For instance, chairs that help frail older adults to stand are helpful for the tired and weary. But because they make standing up easier, many people develop a habit of using the chair riser every time they get up. After awhile, standing up without help ranges from difficult to nearly impossible.

Physical therapy (PT) is a health profession that uses treatments to improve the ability to move, restore function and prevent disability. PT can be helpful with recovery from illness or injury. In the course of most hospital experiences it is possible to have physical therapy. However, when the hospitalization is for a medical problem that does not directly affect joints or bones, PT may not be ordered by your parent's physician unless you ask for it.

Physical therapy can be conducted either in your parent's room or a therapy gym. Therapy will help counter the negative effects of prolonged bed rest. Resistance exercises are the most effective. They require the use of weights, "stretchy" resistance bands or other methods of pushing the muscles to perform.

There are of course times when the severity of illness does not allow exercise and there is little that can be done until your parent's medical condition has stabilized.

In years past, physicians believed that patients needed bed rest to heal. Today quite the opposite has been demonstrated to be true. Getting out of bed as soon as possible – and in most cases within 24 hours after surgery – is more important than bed rest. Even patients who are more seriously ill can benefit from passive movement of their arms and legs.

Standing and walking helps prevent muscle loss and builds strength, but it also has other benefits. Walking around promotes deeper breathing which helps to prevent pneumonia. Patients who move around return to normal bowel function more quickly after surgery or illness. While it may seem counter-intuitive, patients who move around more reduce their need for pain medications more quickly.

Here are some suggestion for what you can do at the hospital and at home:

- Find ways to encourage movement and exercise as soon as your parent's medical condition allows it.

- Ask for a chair in your parent's room so she can get out of bed for part of the day.

- Ask for instructions so you can safely help your parent stand or walk a few steps each time you visit.

- Ask for physical therapy to provide a safe exercise plan including strengthening exercises.

- Encourage your parent to do exercises several times during the day. Work with her to set daily goals for exercise and function. You can start this in the hospital and then continue at home increasing goals as function and strength improve.

- If you and your parent agree to the purchase of a scooter or a rising chair, encourage her to consider her goals when she decides how to use this aid.

- Refer to chapter 5 for more ideas your parent can use to increase strength and mobility when she returns home.

A slip or fall

As you have learned the assumption that institutional settings like hospitals, assisted living, or nursing homes are safe from the risk of falls is wrong. Falls happen in all of these settings.

The hospital will have procedures in place to reduce falls. But that doesn't mean they won't happen. One of the leading causes for older adults ending up at the hospital in the first place is the result of a fall.

Regardless of the reason your parent is in the hospital, a fall in the hospital can be devastating. In addition to the risk for fracture, sutures can be torn lose, internal damage can occur, and recovery can be seriously set back. It is unrealistic to imagine your parent will be safe just because there are healthcare personnel around.

The risk for falls may be one of the reasons hospital staff are reluctant to allow your parent to walk. It is unlikely they have enough staff to routinely help with her exercises or to walk with her multiple times during the day. This is where getting some exercises and advice from a physical therapist is helpful.

Most hospital falls are the result of risk factors that can be known before the fall. This could include weakness, abnormal walking gait, medications that cause dizziness, and altered mental states.

But falls can also occur with patients who do not seem to be at risk for falling. A medical condition can cause unsteadiness, a heart attack or stroke can cause a collapse, or an unexpected response to medications can cause dizziness or a drop in blood pressure. Then there are just plain accidents with no clearly defined cause. Obstacles in the hospital room are common causes of trips and falls.

Confusion, weakness and an unrealistic sense about how ill or frail your parent is in the hospital can lead to her taking chances. A walk to the bathroom can be a mistake before she is ready. Somewhat more complicated are situations when individuals climb over bed rails that were raised for patient safety. This does happen.

What you can do:

- Acknowledge your parent's weakness resulting from illness and hospitalization and talk with her about this.

- Request staff attention to determine the risk for falls and put in place approaches and procedures to decrease the risk for a fall and to increase her strength.

- Look to the recommendations for weakness from bed rest and follow these steps to increase strength and balance.

Delirium, confusion or dementia

Anyone going to an emergency room is likely to experience some confusion. Everything is unknown and strange. The setting is stressful and you are looking for answers to what might be a serious problem. It is a crisis. Otherwise you would not be there. You are confused. Confusion is normal in strange and alien circumstances but sometimes it migrates into a more serious mental terrain known as *delirium*.

The worst thing about delirium, from our perspective here, is that it can present with a set of symptoms not unlike those of *dementia*. Too often hospital staff misdiagnose delirium as dementia. Both conditions are characterized by confusion and an inability to make decisions, among other symptoms. But delirium will clear up once the patient adjusts or is returned to customary surroundings. Dementia does not.

The leap by hospital staff to the label of dementia happens too often. In delirium your parent's mental status will not be normal and she will not be able to make decisions. It is probably caused by the hospitalization, not the kind of cognitive loss that is the defining characteristic of dementia.

Delirium is alarming to anyone not accustomed to seeing it. It develops suddenly often as a concomitant of serious illness, a surgical procedure or hospitalization. It has been estimated that almost half of hospitalized older patients experience some delirium. It can go unrecognized if a patient is quiet and lethargic. Patients who become agitated are more likely to be evaluated for delirium.

Some of the signs of delirium include restlessness, anxiety, irritability, difficulty maintaining attention, changes in sleep patterns, jumbled thinking and communication. In addition, memory loss and confusion about time of day, location or place, and who people are can also lead hospital staff to think the problem is dementia. Family are the ones who can provide critical information.

This is important: *Changes that occur in the hospital but were not present before being in the hospital are most likely delirium, not dementia.*

According to the Mayo Clinic, delirium has many potential causes that are common in a hospital experience. Delirium can be the result of medications that cause disturbance to the chemical balance of the body or by fever or acute infection. It can be caused by metabolic imbalances from changes in nutrition and hydration. Other causes are sleep deprivation, anesthesia affects, and even the loss of normal sensory input due to vision and hearing impairment.

Sometimes delirium affects patients for only a few hours during recovery, but it can go on for weeks or even months. Unmanaged delirium will result in a longer, slower recovery which will impact functional recovery.

Delirium can be managed for recovery; dementia cannot. If delirium is not recognized for what it is and instead is diagnosed as dementia, hospital staff responsible for patient discharge may encourage placement in a secure, specialized dementia care facility rather than a return home. It is your job to be proactive for your parent and see that such a mistake does not happen. If you think she is delirious and not demented, say so. Just raising the issue with staff should result in their reconsideration.

What you can do:

- If you see unusual or confused behavior, ask about delirium.

- Ask questions so you know what will happen each day and explain the plan to your parent as clearly as possible.

- Be aware of the risk for delirium and advocate for your parent, especially if she has reduced mental function.

- Advocate for maintaining a calm environment in your parent's room. Try to limit noise and disruptions to keep the daily schedule as normal as possible.

- Ask about medications and the reason for changes in medication or treatments.

- If sedatives are being given, ask for them to be reduced or eliminated as soon as possible.

- If your parent wears glasses or hearing aids, let staff know where they are and keep them easily available.

Skin breakdown and pressure sores

Anytime there is an illness that results in prolonged bed rest people are at risk for developing sores on their skin. This is particularly true if movement is limited due to severe illness or confinement from something like a cast or special equipment. That said, skin breakdown – typically in the form of pressure sores (more commonly known as bed sores) – is preventable.

Skin breakdown results from sitting or lying in the same position too long. Pressure on the points where the body is touching the bed are the areas of greatest risk. These areas are the parts of the body with the least amount of padding like the elbows, the tailbone, and heels. But any body part that is holding weight against a relatively hard surface can develop a sore. Age, dehydration, and immobility from illness can all increase risk for developing skin breakdowns.

You have probably noticed your parent's skin is more fragile than it used to be. Older people often have bruises and band-aid covered injuries that are the result of the little knocks of daily life.

When you add illness and confinement in a hospital bed the rough sheets and immobility can result in sores on the skin. At first this just looks like a reddened area. If special attention is not provided right away this red area will start to become a sore. Once these sores gets started, they can become very troublesome to heal and often get progressively worse. They are usually painful.

The goal of the hospital care team is to prevent skin breakdown because prevention is much easier to manage than providing the necessary treatment to support the healing of a sore. The nursing staff will work to keep skin clean and dry. They can reduce the risk for skin breakdown through the use of special mattresses, soft cushions and padding. But even with reasonable vigilance pressure sores still happen far too often.

The best way to prevent pressure sores on the skin is for your parent to be repositioned and moved frequently, and for nursing staff to check her skin often.

What you can do:

- If you know your parent has fragile skin, remind nursing staff often. You can also ask about special mattress toppers that are designed to protect skin.

- If you notice that your parent has any red areas, or she comments about areas on her skin that are uncomfortable, bring these to the attention of the nursing staff.

- Ask for a thorough skin evaluation, if you do not know this has been done recently.

- Ask for instructions so you can help your parent move safely, and then help her to move according to these instructions.

- Ask for instructions for the things you can do at home to protect her skin and prevent skin breakdown.

Urgency, frequency and loss of bladder control

Hospital acquired incontinence sounds improbable, yet many older adults who had no urinary incontinence problems before entering the hospital leave in diapers. Not only is this demoralizing, it is not inevitable.

Using a catheter or diapers to capture urine during a serious illness or after a surgery may be necessary for a short period of time. However, the longer a catheter is in place, the harder it will be to remove it and re-establish bladder control. And the longer a person has incontinence, from medical causes or practice, the less likely it can be reversed.

Catheters may be inserted when a patient comes into an emergency department or during a hospital stay. Essentially a catheter is a narrow tube that is inserted into the bladder. It is attached to a bag outside the body that is used to capture urine.

Catheters are easier for staff since they don't have to rush into a room when a patient needs a bedpan or help a patient to get up to use the bathroom. Sometimes insertion of a catheter is almost standard practice for older patients. A catheter may eliminate a wet bed, but it can have serious consequences. If a catheter is used for too long the person may never be free of a catheter or diapers.

In addition, catheter use increases the chances of developing a urinary tract infection. This risk increases every day the catheter remains in place. If the bacteria causing the infection are resistant to antibiotic treatment, the infection can become very serious leading to kidney infection or worse.

A study of catheter use in the emergency room setting found that there was no clear reason for one of every three patients who had a catheter inserted. Strikingly this study found that for women over 80, half of those who were catheterized did not meet the clinical guidelines for a catheter. While all patients over 80 were much more likely to have a catheter inserted, women were at a higher risk for unnecessary catheterization.

Once a catheter is inserted it needs to be re-evaluated as soon as possible. In a hospital, as shifts of clinical staff change and a patient is moved from one unit to another, the catheter becomes just another part of the care plan. The care plan may not include evaluation for its removal until days have past. If someone in the emergency department inserted the catheter, the hospital physician may not consider it important to evaluate the continued use as focus on other clinical care needs take priority. Nurses and doctors in the hospital are focused on the management of medical problems and often don't pay attention to the life-altering consequences of allowing, or even encouraging, incontinence.

Consider the older woman who had a catheter inserted in the hospital just because she had problems with urgency. She didn't know very long in advance when she would need to go to the bathroom. When she did she would press the call button and wait. But patient care staff would arrive too late. When this happened once too often, a catheter was inserted.

Then staff would tell her, no need to call us, just go ahead and urinate whenever you need to go. She complained and was told not to worry about it. Then when she left the hospital she was put in adult diapers. So she arrived at the nursing home for rehabilitation with diapers. No one questioned this. Her chart probably reflected incontinence as just one of her clinical problems.

She continued to complain but was told "just go when you need to."

By the time she was back home again, she had lost bladder control. This made her depressed and demoralized. The home care aides just handled the diapers as the way things were and there was no attempt to help her regain bladder control.

You may need to be insistent about your concerns regarding the risks of catheter use. All hospitals are short staffed with nursing staff stretched to meet the demands of clinical care. They may not be eager to add to their workload when the catheter saves them time. But if you bring the problem to their attention they are likely to work with your parent to resolve the problem before discharge.

If your attempts are unsuccessful and your parent leaves the hospital with a new incontinence problem there are still things you both can do to make this a temporary situation.

Start by keeping track of the time of day when incontinence occurs. Perhaps this is an hour after your parent's morning cup of coffee for example. Or perhaps this is when she gets up to take a walk or do exercises.

Do not make the mistake of thinking that cutting back on fluids is the answer to this problem. It is not. That would only put your parent at risk for dehydration, bladder infections, skin breakdown, and other problems.

Once you have established the times when incontinence typically occurs, you can start a bathroom schedule. For example, if you learn that incontinence is likely at certain times of day or with certain activities, you can plan a trip to the bathroom right before this time. Over time, more and more control will return with more successful trips to the bathroom and fewer wet diapers. At the same time your parent will benefit emotionally with improved self-esteem.

As a final point, sometimes incontinence is preferable to the loss of independent living. If your parent is at home, she may decide that wearing diapers is preferred to the risks of walking to the bathroom on her own when no one is there. Make it her choice, not something you mandate, and it will be easier for her to accept.

What you can do if your parent has a catheter inserted during a hospital stay:

- Don't be complacent. Ask every day about the plans to remove the catheter.

- Ask for a bladder evaluation.

- Ask for a plan to prevent incontinence when the catheter is removed including a bladder training program.

- Be insistent about your concerns.

What you can do at home if your parent is incontinent:

- Track the times when incontinence happens and plan trips to the bathroom at regular intervals.

- Focus the location of your parent's activities near a bathroom when possible.

- Obtain a bedside commode for use during the night.

- Ask your parent's doctor about Kegel exercises and work with your parent to do these exercises frequently during the day.[24] (Kegel exercises have been shown to help both men and women to reduce incontinence.)

Pills, pills, and more pills

Older adults take more medications than any other age group and as people age the number of medications increases. Each new chronic illness results in more medications. The result is that many older adults take ten or more medications. Each additional medication increases the risk for interactions with other medications.

When I was advisor to the Health Foundation in New York several studies were commissioned to learn about the problems associated with medications. It was learned that adverse drug events can lead to hospitalization. After being hospitalized, one in five hospital re-admissions within a month after discharge are the result of medication problems.

Broadly adverse medication events occur anytime there is harm caused by a medication or the absence of a needed medication. This harm can be the result of a reaction to a medication such as a side effect, allergy or other reaction. Or the result when a medication is not taken as it was planned. If you make sure prior to leaving the hospital that you understand the medications your parent takes – both why and how they should be taken – that can reduce the likelihood of her being re-hospitalized.

Earlier I mentioned the Beers List of Medications. This list was put together by the American Geriatrics Society to advise physicians regarding medications that can cause problems in older adults. Many older adults are taking medications on the list. Balancing the benefits and risks is an important consideration.

Pain pills prescribed after surgery are typically narcotics or opioids. While they are effective in managing post surgical pain, these drugs have risks. The drugs can cause complications in healing and increase the risk of falling with a side effect of dizziness. They can also cause constipation which can be hazardous and painful. Prolonged use of these drugs is also addicting. Changing to non-narcotic pain medication and other methods of pain relief can support faster recovery after surgery.

During a stay in the hospital it is also possible for new medications to create unexpected problems. A new medication might treat the new diagnosis, but cause a problem with some other drug your parent takes. This drug interaction can cause a change in how your parent feels. It can make her feel worse or even lead to a more serious complication. She could even experience a drug allergy that wasn't previously known.

Finally, it is possible that everything in the plan is good, but when medications are given there is an error in dosage or administration. A wrong dose can even be deadly in some cases. More than 95 percent of hospitals now use electronic medical records and automated drug dispensing. The accuracy of prescription drug orders and providing individual medication has improved significantly as a result. In addition to rapid exchange of important information, the electronic documentation systems also have the ability to check for interactions between drugs and other potential risks.

When a person is hospitalized it is not unusual for medications to be changed. Sometimes there is a change to a similar medication and sometimes medications are added to treat the reason for the admission. When it is time to go back home some hospitals will provide a review of these medications to be sure patients have an accurate list of what should be taken when they return home. This is good practice. A review of medications prior to discharge can remove the medications that were given in the hospital and identify the ones that should not be continued after discharge.

The significance of potential harm from medications means that vigilance is needed by patients and families.

What you can you do:

- Ask about medications that are given to your parent. Question any that you don't understand or that doesn't look familiar.

- Ask for narcotic medications to be changed to non-narcotic pain medications as soon as it is reasonable to do so.

- Call attention to any changes in how your parent feels, behaves or communicates when medications are changed. Keep in mind that even a change in medications within the same class of drug or a change in manufacturer of a drug can change how it affects your parent.

- Request a medication review before your parent is discharged. Be sure both you and she ask questions so that you understand *what* medications should be taken, *when* they should be taken, and *how* they should be taken. Also clarify which medications are no longer needed.

Medical errors

Some years ago a major study by the Institute of Medicine[25] brought attention to the problem of human error in medicine. Since that time hospitals have made quite a few changes to reduce the chances of making errors. This has served to improve the odds in favor of patients.

When your parent goes into a medical facility for treatment or some procedure, medical personnel will ask for her name at every step of the way and sometimes mark her body to indicate the spot where the procedure will be focused. This can become annoying, but it is important to prevent operating on the wrong person or body part.

Recently there has been a closer look at accuracy of medical diagnosis, or the process necessary to determine the nature of one's medical problem. Diagnosis is a complex process that can involve a series of laboratory and technical procedures. The process can rely on numerous individuals completing these tests and procedures to provide the physician with information necessary to make a decision regarding the problem – to give the new problem a medical diagnosis.

According to the Institute of Medicine, medical error is a failure of accuracy and timely identification of a patient's health problem. Included is the failure to explain the medical problem clearly to the patient.

Their definition reflects both the complexity of identification of medical problems as well as the need to explain the diagnosis. Sometimes medical errors occur when there are problems in the communication between physicians and others providing care, or between the medical staff and the patients and family.

Every licensed healthcare organization will have procedures in place to reduce the risk of errors during the diagnostic process, but errors can still happen. The doctors who provide treatment in an emergency department or other parts of the hospital are not likely to know your parent. Thus they will be unaware of her medical problems or other aspects of her healthcare history. That makes it more difficult for them to catch discrepancies.

Not even electronic medical records can prevent all errors when doctors need to act quickly in complex or critical situations. Doctors will respond to what they see. They don't have time to delve into a patient's history. Both emergency room doctors and those in the hospital are trained to identify problems quickly and respond with appropriate treatment quickly.

The systems of hospital and medical care can also contribute to medical errors both by creating barriers to communication with families and because the culture of medicine discourages disclosure when there are errors. Errors in diagnosis can lead to delays in appropriate treatment. Errors can also lead to unnecessary or even potentially harmful treatments. These problems are so common it is probable that most of us will experience an error in diagnosis at some time during our lifetime. But there are some things you can do to help to ensure your parent does not experience an error in medical diagnosis or procedure when she is in the hospital. The most important thing is to listen and ask questions. Make sure you understand what your parent's physician thinks her problem is.

Press for the details even though you might not understand the medical jargon. Write down what you hear. Ask for the correct spelling of terms. Then later you can search reliable sites on the internet to get a better understanding of the information you have been told. Keeping a written record of what happens in the hospital will help you advocate for your parent's care. Later your notes will help you explain to her what happened there.

One of the key recommendations in the Institute report was to improve communication at all levels. While the report focused on the communication by physicians with patients and the communication between the various people involved in the diagnostic process, it also speaks to the importance of the patient's role in communication.

Although there is always some risk of being labeled a "difficult" patient or family member, you have the right, and indeed the responsibility, to ask questions. Work to understand your parent's medical condition. If you get labeled difficult, so be it.

Even with an accurate diagnosis the treatment plan might not adhere to the best standards of care. Sometimes staff make incorrect assumptions about the abilities of a patient or family caregiver. Sometimes the treatment for one condition might be at cross purposes with the treatment for another.

Consider, for example, a patient who is hard of hearing. If a person cannot hear instructions they are unlikely to be followed. Again, it is important for an older patient to have someone who can listen to the instructions given and write them down, as well as speak for the patient to advocate for their interests.

What you can do:

- Do not assume that just because your parent is in a good hospital there will be no errors. Bad things can happen in the best of institutions. Stay alert.

- If you think something is wrong, or if your parent's condition is worsening, bring it to the attention of nursing staff and doctor.

- Make notes about treatments and results.

- Ask why a test or procedure is needed and what risks are involved.

- Ask questions – repeatedly if necessary – until you understand a planned treatment, its expected outcome, and its risks.

- Ask about treatment options and how they compare for both benefits and risks.

Malnutrition and dehydration

Patients are sometimes admitted to the hospital in a state of malnutrition. In fact some studies have shown that more than half of newly hospitalized older adults are malnourished. Older adults who get and prepare their own food may not get enough to eat. Grocery costs are a factor for some but there are many other reasons why so many elderly people are ill-fed and malnourished.

Some of the reasons are practical, such as difficulty getting to a grocery store or managing once they are there. Many also buy pre-prepared foods because they are easier. These kinds of food often have high salt and fat content, and lower nutritional value. Older people may no longer eat regular meals as the result of social isolation, loss of a spouse, depression or other mental health issues.

Most patients are evaluated for their nutritional status upon admission to a hospital. But be aware that even if your parent is identified as dehydrated or undernourished this does not mean the care plan will include a focus on improving her nutritional status while she is in the hospital.

It seems unthinkable that a patient could practically starve in a hospital or struggle with being thirsty. But it happens all too often. Adequate food and fluids are important for healing but in the daily routine of a busy hospital it might not be a high priority.

Another factor is the requirement that patients fast prior to certain diagnostic tests, procedures or surgeries. Delays in any of these procedures can result in long periods of time without food or drink.

While there are standards for the development and preparation of numerous *special* diets prepared by the hospital, there are no universally applied nutrition standards to ensure patients consume meals. So patients might be served adequate food that they cannot or will not eat.

Chronic medical conditions may cause loss of appetite and swallowing problems that interfere with eating and drinking. Interest in eating can also be affected by food selection that may be different from the foods one eats at home. This is made worse when a person eats an ethnic diet at home and is given standard American food in the hospital. Or maybe the special diet provided just doesn't taste appealing to the individual. All of these possibilities can lead to some level of malnutrition.

Hospital staff focused on the management of acute medical conditions don't pay much attention to how much and what the patient eats. Meal trays are put in front of the patient and later someone comes to pick them up again. Someone may document how much is eaten but little else.

If a patient needs some assistance with opening containers, cutting food into bites or other assistance, there may not be staff available to provide this personal attention. Water may be left on the bedside cabinet, out of a patient's reach. If a patient has difficulty eating regular meals, nursing staff might bring juice, Jello or pudding between meals. What the person really needs is protein interspersed throughout the day to help healing, support normal functioning, and retain strength.

Hospitals have guidelines for ensuring adequate protein is included in meals, but that doesn't mean that anyone is making sure that your parent is eating the egg and not just the toast and jam for breakfast.

What you can do:

- Plan your visits around meal times and help your parent reach her food.

- Encourage your parent to eat some of everything, not just the foods that taste best to her.

- Ask for additional beverages and snacks between meals. Keep water or other beverages within reach.

- If your parent has difficulty swallowing, ask for thickened liquids and nectar-like juices.

- Ask if you can bring healthy snacks, beverages and foods that are familiar to your parent.

- Plan to ensure your parent will have food in her house when she returns home or make sure that home-delivered meals are part of her discharge plan.

Another few words about artificial hydration and nutrition. Sometime in the course of your parent's care, or perhaps as she nears the end of her life, you may be asked to make a decision regarding the use of artificial hydration and nutrition. Before that time comes review the longer discussion on this topic in chapter 8. If your parent is no longer able to make this decision on her own, you will only be allowed to make a decision against artificial hydration or nutrition if she has included on her healthcare power of attorney form that her agent knows her wishes about artificial hydration and nutrition. It is up to you to speak up for your parent's wishes according to how they are documented on her advance directive forms.

Feelings of loss, isolation and depression

One of the risks of hospitalization that seems obvious, but is often overlooked, is the psychological impact of hospitalization. This is particularly significant if your parent has some cognitive decline. A sense of loss and isolation can lead to depression.

Your parent is away from her home, her routine and many of the things most meaningful to her. She is being cared for by an ever changing group of people who may well be competent and caring, but they are strangers. The hospital is noisy so it is hard to sleep, yet she drifts in and out of naps. Day and night can become confused.

Your parent may also be uncertain about her health status and her ability to ever return home. If she doesn't understand the reasons for hospitalization or the treatments, this will add to her concerns. She may be concerned about things that don't even make sense to you. She may miss the view from her kitchen window or the meals-on-wheels delivery person. Everything is strange. New. Confusing. It's hard to focus on the work of getting well.

People experience stress, especially in uncertain situations, in different ways. Illness and the physical impact including potential loss of function are difficult to handle by almost everyone. Confinement in a hospital bed can lead to feelings of helplessness as the most basic of daily care requires the help of others. This is made especially onerous because they are strangers.

When care is provided it can feel pretty impersonal, even with the best attempts on the part of staff to be caring in their approach. Staff in healthcare settings are also notorious for appearing to be in a hurry. This can make a person feel that someone else's care and needs are more important.

Many older patients report that the favorite phrase of hospital staff is "I'll be right back" But then the person is not right back. This can reduce self worth. Sometimes it leads to depression. The symptoms of this might be changes in appetite, difficulty sleeping, fatigue, an overall sense of hopelessness and withdrawal.

With the hospital staff narrowly focused on the reason for the hospital admission – and the fact that they don't know your parents temperament and personality – means these changes in mental health can easily be missed. They might just think she is an old woman with some cognitive loss. They may not realize that normally she is active, articulate, capable and cheerful.

What you can do:

- Without interfering with necessary medical care, ensure the presence of caring family and friends every day. Make sure your parent does not feel abandoned.

- Watch for changes in affect and behavior. Inform staff if you detect unusual reactions that might get in the way of recovery.

- Work with your parent and her care team to prepare for discharge with a plan based on her goals and adequate steps to reach those goals.

- Encourage your parent to participate, and her care team to include her, in care planning. Urge them to allow her as much control as possible.

Unwanted or inappropriate treatment

Previous chapters discussed the likelihood that care plans will result in recommendations for treatment that your parent may not want. While this was discussed in detail it is a problem so significant it bears repeating.

The dwindles can last for eight years or more with several dips and rises in condition over time. It is difficult to decide that the current dip is the one that will lead to the end of life. While unnecessary care at the end of life isn't quite the same as some of the other hazards of hospitalization, it continues to be a problem. Family caregivers should keep it in mind when considering treatment choices.

Hospital-based physicians tend to overestimate the positive results possible from treatments, including the impact on quality of life and future functional ability. Thus they might bypass less aggressive treatment in favor of a more aggressive treatment because that is recommended by a clinical guideline.

It is not only in the U.S. that this is a problem. An international study looked at the care of 1.2 million people and found the problem to be worldwide. New treatments are often started in the last six months of life, even when the treatment will make no difference to the outcome of the illness.

Not all of the blame for inappropriate treatment can be assigned to healthcare professionals. Families are sometimes unrealistic about what can be done successfully. Family members often just cannot accept

Chapter 14. Ten common hazards of hospitalization... 225

that their loved one is near the end of life. They are no doubt influenced by television programs, movies and books that depict miracle recoveries in what seemed like hopeless circumstances. The hero, near death from multiple gun shot wounds, comes to in the hospital, disdainfully disconnects himself from the monitors and goes out and gets the bad guys. That might be interesting and make for a more exciting fictional drama, but it does not happen that way in real life.

It is difficult for a family member to accept that further treatment will only delay the inevitable. They cannot accept the advice that further attempts at care or treatment will only make dying worse for their loved one.

Sometimes toward the end comfort care or palliative care is the best, perhaps the only realistic option. That does not mean no care. It just means decisions made will focus on things that generally aren't very high tech. This could include managing pain or providing spiritual or emotional support. The transition between a focus on cure and survival to palliative care may be gradual and is not just an either-or situation.

Here is a reminder of what you can do:

- Make sure your parent is in possession of her advance directive documents when she goes to the hospital.

- Ask that her advance directive document be entered into her medical record.

- Make arrangements to either be with your parent when she goes to the hospital or to have someone she trusts with her to help her speak up for care choices.

- Participate in critical medical decisions, even when your parent is able to speak for herself. Ask questions to understand the treatment choices, the likely benefit and the potential risks.

- Rehearse the way you will express your parent's opinions in the event you need to say no to proposed treatments.

Hospitals are remarkable places. They are full of high tech equipment and talented, experienced medical personnel. They can quickly assess the medical needs of patients and respond with fast, effective treatments. And many hospitals work to create an environment that supports healing. They recognize the importance of paying attention to more than the physical illnesses and injuries that bring patients to the hospital.

At the same time hospitals are very large, fast moving places. They are staffed by many people trained to provide an almost bewildering array of services, all focused on meeting the needs of a rapidly changing population of patients. Your understanding and awareness of some of the things that can go wrong will empower you as part of your parent's care team. You know your parent, her values and her goals better than anyone else at the hospital. You can make observations that others might miss and keep her goals in focus. Together with her medical team you can help your parent leave the hospital on the road to recovery.

Notes

[24] Kegel exercises are repeated contracting and relaxing the muscles that are known as the pelvic floor. These muscles can prevent incontinence

[25] The Institute of Medicine is a nonprofit organization that functions as a part of the US National Academy of Sciences. It works independently of the government to conduct research and recommendations for health policy.

15
Post-hospitalization complications and how to avoid them

TREATMENT IN A HOSPITAL can have its hazards but is sometimes unavoidable. A hospital is still the best place to manage an urgent or serious medical problem. Ironically, at the end of a parent's hospital care it might seem that it ended too soon. Don't be surprised if your parent does not feel like he is ready to go home. It is often said that patients leave the hospital quicker and sicker.

Today patients remain in a hospital only as long as its high level of service and expertise are needed. It is quite likely that your parent will need continued help for a while after she returns home from a hospital stay.

Because of the many risks associated with a stay in the hospital, it is hard to argue against going home as soon as possible. But it does mean that you and other family members will be expected to provide more care than you might have expected. Most family members are willing to provide care but feel unprepared.

Instructions will be provided at the hospital and there will be written instructions in the materials provided as part of the discharge process. Hospital staff should go over these materials with you and your parent before final discharge. Assumptions are made. You might not be asked if you are willing and able to provide the care your parent will need. You will find it a stressful time trying to understand many things that are unfamiliar and to learn what needs to be done to support your parent's recovery. If you do not fully understand the instructions, ask questions until you do. Don't take your parent home from the hospital unsure of what you are supposed to do next.

The movement from one care setting to another is called *care transition*. Researchers have have found that this time of hand-off or care transition is challenging and risky. So this is a time to be especially alert.

It is likely that more than one hospital staff person will give you discharge instructions. You will be told what to expect when you get home, any treatments that should be followed, precautions regarding activities, special dietary needs, perhaps some exercises to be done for recovery, how medications have changed, follow-up appointments, and anything else relative to your parent's care.

When your parent leaves the hospital she will be given a *discharge summary* that should include recommendations for post-hospital care. The discharge instructions for care may be mixed in with a lot of other paperwork. Look for them before you leave the hospital. They might not be easy to understand. Fortunately this, too, is changing for the better. Most hospitals now print out the instructions (they used to commonly be hand written). But they still may not be stated clearly enough for you to understand what they say. Read them closely – again, before you leave – and question anything you don't understand.

The discharge information packet should include a summary of the care your parent received in the hospital. There might also be brochures with information about potentially helpful community services.

Hospitals know that care transitions are challenging. This is a problem that some of them try to solve by throwing a lot of information at the patient and family. This can make the transition even more overwhelming.

If the discharge packet contains more literature than you can reasonably sift through before leaving, ask someone at the hospital to point out the most important information. Expect them to do the sifting for you; it's their job. Most will be happy to help. Ask them to identify the *critical* information you will need to support your parent during her first few days at home.

Also look in the discharge package for the date and time of a follow-up appointment with your parent's primary physician. Then, go through the packet again as soon as possible after you get your parent home.

Because it is rare for primary care physicians to see patients in the hospital, it is important that your parent sees her physician very soon after she is discharged from the hospital.

Sharing the information from the hospital admission with her doctor will help ensure that ongoing treatment plans will improve your parent's health and function. Even though it may seem a burden to plan a physician appointment soon after your parent returns home, it is important. Without this reconnection your parent is at higher risk of being advised to return to the hospital if her condition changes.

Several groups and physicians across the country have been working to understand what happens during typical transitions of care. They have identified the risks for the patients during these transitions. From this understanding they have developed approaches to support patients and families to minimize the negative aspects of the transfer. As these efforts have shown their effectiveness, they are gradually spreading across the country.

The first and biggest problem is a breakdown in communication. Hospital staff may do an admirable job of describing what will happen next and the expectations for care at home. But this is often shared quite rapidly. The staff will ask family if they understand, and if they have any questions. Family members often just nod even when they really don't understand.

A better approach is when the hospital staff person asks you to repeat the instructions back. This has proven to be a good practice and you should appreciate when you are asked to repeat instructions. If you are not asked, you can always say, "Let me repeat those instructions back to you to be sure I haven't missed anything." This is particularly important with medications and any treatments that will be your responsibility to provide. You should also make sure you include how to manage such things as dressings, drainage containers, splints and how to administer various medications.

A common problem that arises is when a hospital staff person gives discharge instructions to your parent when you aren't there. Try to avoid this by making it clear that you want to be included when discharge instructions are reviewed. But be aware that this is no guarantee that it won't happen anyway. Lots of people are involved in the care of a patient in the hospital and the person who actually provides the discharge instructions may never know about your request. The electronic medical records can flag important family caregiver relationships, but don't count on staff remembering to schedule at a time that works for you. If this happens and you do get left out, get someone to repeat the discharge instructions for you.

Somewhere in this process it is important for you to be clear about what you are able and willing to do to help your parent when she gets home. Several times over the years I have heard family members say something like, "I was so glad when my husband came home from the hospital, but I was not prepared for _____" The unprepared-for task is usually something the person considers unpleasant, like changing a dressing, caring for a drainage tube, or help in bathing.

Hopefully the hospital staff will ask you what you are willing and able to do, but they might not. If you are unable to handle some of the necessary care because of other demands on your time, your physical abilities, or just because it seems icky or too intimate, you need to speak up.

If your parent was in the hospital long enough to qualify for it, Medicare-covered home care can be a solution. A large number of eligible patients are sent home without anyone considering the option to engage home care services. If a specific nursing or rehabilitation need exists, then home care is more likely to be put into place. If you think your parent will need help at home ask for home health to be included in the discharge plan. But, be aware that it may take a couple of days for home care services to begin.

Another part of the problem with communication is that information doesn't always get to the next care providers. This can actually start as a problem in the hospital if your parent is moved from one unit to another or is sent to another part of the hospital for a procedure. All of the important information may not get to the new staff. With so many people and departments involved in providing care, it is actually amazing that more gaps don't occur. If you are keeping track and have copies of instructions you can help bridge this gap.

There are a few options at discharge. These days most patients go directly home from the hospital. If your parent will receive home care this will include transferring care to a home health agency. Or, your parent may go to a nursing home rehabilitation unit for a few days or weeks to regain strength and mobility. In either of these situations your parent's care is being transferred to a new agency. The potential for communication problems magnify.

The home health agency or nursing home will receive a summary of her full condition, her medical status, her treatment requirements, and her medications. Before the new agency can begin providing care a physician is required to make new medical orders. This will be a new physician who won't know your parent and opens the door to potential communication problems during the care transition.

Information provided to the next point of care may not be presented in a way that new staff can make the most use of the information. Sometimes the information is a poor reproduction and hard to read on a duplicate copy. Sometimes the important information is lost within a stack of paperwork. As the family caregiver, if you have been keeping track of your parent's care and have a copy of the discharge plan you can help make sure the important information is not lost.

Chapter 15. Post-hospitalization complications... 235

The hospital may not provide the information quickly to your parent's personal physician. The physician may not know your parent was in the hospital, much less why, or what was recommended at her discharge. It may be up to you to provide this information.

To understand the potential problem that can arise from not getting the right information to the next step in care, here is an example. A care transitions project I led several years ago included a team that wanted to make sure the right information went with nursing home residents to the hospital emergency room. The team was composed of hospital emergency and nursing home staff. They looked at the information that the nursing home typically put together and found that 40 pages of information were the average. In addition to the critical medical information they included social history and other documents the staff thought important. After their work together with the hospital they were able to hone down to the more critical information in eight pages.

Here is how things typically worked *before* the project. When the nursing home copied forty pages to send, the actual patient's transport was delayed while someone made photocopies of all the required documents. Then the emergency room staff ignored most of what was sent because they were in a hurry. They did not have time to read through it all to find the information they needed. Clinical decisions were made based on what the emergency room doctors saw when they evaluated the patient.

Documents that were too long and detailed opened up the opportunity for lots of things to go wrong. But getting down to essential information helped the hospital doctors and staff make quicker decisions. This led to better results.

But – and here is the critical point from a caregiver's perspective – making the document shorter resulted in the omission of much of the patient's background information. A lot had to be left out that described who the person was. What emergency room staff need is much different from the requirements for a more general scope of care. The big picture is focused more narrowly for an immediate need, but if the big picture is lost, care down the road will suffer. You must keep this kind of focus-refocus in mind and always remain alert to the many opportunities for error. Anticipate what you can and plan ahead for the next step in your parent's care and recovery.

The importance of medication management has been discussed previously. Post-hospital medications can be a common care-transition problem. If your parent has had surgery, for example, make sure she has the pain medication she will need. The hospital staff might be so busy getting your parent ready for discharge that they forget to give her a pain pill before she leaves. If she is sent to a nursing home for rehabilitation care they will not be able to give her any medications until they get new doctor's orders.

Avoid this kind of situation by requesting your parent be given a pain pill before you leave the hospital. You can also ask for discharge medication to take with you. Discharge medications are provided most often for patients who are going home and would find it difficult to stop at a pharmacy on the way. You can ask for discharge medications when your parent is leaving the hospital for any new care setting. Most will be able to comply with your request.

As noted earlier it would not be a surprise if the hospital doctors added some new medications during the hospitalization. Or, perhaps not new, but they look different, which can make them seem new. Sometimes pills have a similar purpose but different name. These and other sources of confusion can lead to serious mistakes in taking the medications. Complications with medications can result in your parent ending up right back in the hospital.

Medication problems from wrong doses, to missed doses, to duplicate medications, and more, are a major reason why older patients have to be re-admitted to the hospital within weeks of discharge. So before your parent leaves the hospital be certain you understand the medications she should take at home.

Another gap to be concerned about during a care transition is the disruption in access to food and fluids. The discharge from the hospital or rehabilitation setting may conflict with meal delivery so your parent may be sent on her way having missed a meal. If she arrives at the next place of care after mealtime she can miss a second meal.

Some hospitals are creative about this and send a meal along with the discharged patient. If you request something like this you might get a meal-to-go.

If your parent goes home from the hospital, she may have an empty fridge. There might not be anything to eat in her home. The home health nurse will check to make sure your parent has food in the house, but that might not be for a day or two.

Some community aging services have volunteer programs to bring a small amount of groceries to a home after discharge but these programs are rare. As your parent's family caregiver, making sure your parent has food and something to drink after she leaves the hospital is one more thing you might need to take care of yourself.

One of the leading physicians in the country who is working to improve care transitions is Dr. Eric Coleman. While we were conducting a large project together I had a chance to hear him talk about the importance of older adults and their caregivers becoming prepared and taking responsibility.

Dr. Coleman shares with healthcare professionals facts to help them understand the importance of ensuring understanding among patients and their families when they leave the hospital. As he reminds them, the only constant in a transition from one care setting to another is the patient. Everyone and everything else are variable.

Even with care provided by a home health agency in the home, the bulk of care is still provided by the patient herself or by her family.

He explains this in a very practical way. Consider how many hours there are in a week (168). If your parent sees a physician for 20 minutes and a home care nurse is in her home twice for 30 minutes each time, that is a total time of an hour and twenty minutes with a healthcare professional. That leaves all of the remaining 166 hours and 40 minutes in the hands of you, your parent and family caregivers.

If you are the one who will be in the primary role to support your parent's recovery after a hospital stay, these numbers show how critical the role is. This points out why it is so important that you ask all of the questions you need to ask so you understand every aspect of your responsibility. It is vital that you comprehend – at a layman's level – your parent's medical problems and what you can do to help her stay as healthy and functional as possible.

Don't rely on healthcare teams making sure you know what you need to know to care for your parent. Take it upon yourself to make certain you are prepared for the responsibility.

Challenge the assumption that you are prepared. Assume that your parent's doctor is not informed about her hospitalization. Assume that any new care providers do not have the information they need.

Don't be afraid to ask questions and don't hesitate to speak up if you do not:

- think your parent's wishes are being considered in the discharge planning process;

- understand your parent's medications or their care instructions; or

- understand when your parent needs to be seen by her various care providers.

Next Step in Care™ is a useful website[26] that offers numerous tools and resources to help your parent have the most successful transition possible. The resources on this site were developed from experience working with family caregivers over many years. They recognized that families need better resources to clarify the sometimes confusing steps in care and to help them take more prepared responsibility.

The *Next Step in Care* site has a series of guides on such things as the medical privacy law HIPAA, medication management, what you need to do to prepare both for your parent's hospitalization, and for her next step in care. These guides are available in several languages and are easy to understand and use.

Hopefully, the best result has occurred after the medical crisis and hospitalization and your parent will now be on the path to recovery.

The next chapter summarizes the content of this book with practical steps and ideas to help you and your parent create a three-pillared system for successful care at home.

Notes

[26]Next Step in Care website: www.nextstepincare.org A practical, easy to use website full of guides to help older adults and their families manage the various aspects of healthcare with an emphasis on support through transitions of care from one setting to another. The website was developed by the United Hospital Fund in New York City.

16
The three pillars of all-in caregiving

Put together the information from this book using organization and the three pillars of all-in caregiving: *medication management, personal health record* and a *Go Folder*. They can help you and your parent manage her health. As you know by now the amount of information provided by medical services and pharmacies can seem daunting. With a bit of organization you can manage it all.

Medication management

Medication management is one of the most important caregiver tasks. Failure to do it well risks a decline in your parent's health status. It is also a frequent reason people end up in the hospital. Once you have a good system for managing medications that works for you and for your parent, adding the other pieces becomes much easier.

There are, at a minimum, four steps you should take in order to start and maintain good medication management.

Step One: *Understand the* what, why, when *and* how *of each medication.*

Medication prescriptions can come from any and all of your parent's doctors. Effective and safe medication management starts with understanding each of these medications. Your parent should understand them as well as she is able.

Some of the more important considerations are:

- What does each medication look like?

- When and how should it be taken?

- What side effects should we be concerned about?

- What side effects should her doctor be told about?

- Are there serious side effects that call for immediate medical treatment if they occur? Remember the idea of recognizing red flags.

Not all answers have to come from your parent's doctor. Pharmacists are excellent resources. When you pick up any prescription you will be asked if you want to talk with the pharmacist. Some pharmacies require speaking with the pharmacist when you pick up any prescription.

The most frequent question when you pick up a prescription is likely to be, "Do you have any questions?" That is not an idle question so don't shrug it off. The easy answer is "no." After all, it is just a bottle of small pills. What's there to ask?

Or you might be planning on reading the information the pharmacy provides with each medication. There is plenty of it. There is the drug company insert, usually lots of words in small type, giving details about potential side effects, drug study results, and on and on. Pharmacists know that very few people will actually read these things so they provide their own (usually) briefer summary information with details about the medication.

You should read everything. Carefully. Take notes. Research the terms you don't know or understand. All that printed material probably provides the answers to all your questions.

Evidently most people don't read very much about the medications they take. But even if you are a scholar and plan to read everything, you should still question the pharmacist about the "important considerations" listed above. Make sure you have a clear understanding of the medication before your parent starts using it. The pharmacist might also have some tips and information not mentioned in the literature you receive.

There are often special instructions about when or how a medication should be taken. With certain medications, for example, it is important to drink a full glass of water with a pill. For some it is important to take with food, while another might best be taken before food. With some drugs it is important to stay upright for awhile, while others might specifically call for the avoidance of a particular food or supplement. There are many possible special conditions and requirements. A brief conversation with the pharmacist can give you the most important ones.

You may discover that your parent will not take a medication. Perhaps it is too much trouble or maybe it causes an unpleasant side effect. Understanding more about each medication will help you encourage her to talk with her doctor about why she doesn't want to take a medication as prescribed. A pharmacist can help with this too. Your parent might be more comfortable telling the pharmacist why she doesn't want to take the medication as prescribed. The pharmacist may be the one who can call the physician to find another option that is easier for your parent to manage.

If your parent is experiencing an unpleasant side effect, the pharmacist may have a suggestion to ease the condition. My husband was prescribed an inhaler but it caused him to lose his voice so he stopped using it. When asked, the pharmacist explained that this is a common side effect and a simple gargle with water after using the inhaler usually lessened the problem. It worked. Now he breathes better and still has a strong voice. So ask questions to be sure you understand how each medication should be taken.

If you notice a change in condition, even if it is just a seemingly minor change in attitude or behavior, the first question to ask is whether your parent is taking a new medication or taking an old medication differently.

As was pointed out earlier, it is not unusual for older adults to take five or more different medications. Side effects can become more complex as new medications are added. Drugs interact. The more medications a person takes, the more likely there will be an unexpected drug interaction. Sometimes side effects can be reduced if the interacting medications are taken at different times of the day. A pharmacist can help figure out the best way to minimize side effects.

Negative consequences of prescriptions are not limited to how they interact with each other. Remember, there are some medications that have increased risks when taken by older adults.

For example, some medications can increase the risk of a fall. High blood pressure is a problem that affects three of every four people over 70 years of age. Treating high blood pressure, while very important, can also increase the risk for falls. A fall with injury can have just as much impact on a person's life as a stroke or heart attack. So what's a person to do? You certainly don't want your parent to suffer a fall. But you also want to prevent a heart attack or stroke.

This is a good discussion to have together with your parent's doctor. If your parent becomes dizzy when she stands up or has become confused, her doctor may want to make adjustments to her medication or the time of day when she takes it. The goal is to find a good balance between risks and benefits.

By the way, it is okay to ask about the cost of medications. Each Medicare Part D medication plan has a different list of covered medications. You may find the prescribed medication is covered but it has a higher cost than a similar medication in the same group. If you ask about cost, the lower cost medication in the group can be selected.

Step Two: *Develop a process to keep track of medications and their schedule.*

To organize your parent's medications and keep track of when they should be taken, your parent should have a complete list of every medication she takes. She will benefit from doing this herself but you might have to help. Start with the list from her doctor's visit summary. Before you set up a schedule you want to make sure you have everything on the list.

Set all of your parent's medications on a table. Include everything she takes regularly regardless of whether it was prescribed by a physician or it is something she chooses to take. Include vitamins, herbs, antacids, pain killers and every other over-the-counter medication your parent takes, either regularly or occasionally.

Read the instructions on each medication. For each one write down the dose such as milligrams (mg), milliliters (ml) or drops. Note when the medication is to be taken, whether she needs to eat some food with it or any other requirements, why it is taken, which doctor told her to take the medication and when she starting taking it. Use what you learn to develop a list of everything your parent takes. (See appendix A for a medication list template.)

Before you start writing you might find it helpful to group medications together on the table according to when they are taken. This makes it easier when you enter them on a list.

You may find when you set out all of the medications that the instructions require medications to be taken frequently throughout the day. To take everything as planned, your parent's daily routine becomes one of keeping track of when to take various medications.

Several physicians and pharmacists I have worked with believe too many seniors needlessly complicate their lives with medication-taking routines that look like airport flight schedules. Most people can group their medications into no more than four times a day (morning, noon, dinnertime, and bedtime). Find the lowest number of different times of the day as possible.

You may want to change when or how your parent takes a medication to minimize their impact on her daily life. Be sure to review your plan with her doctor or pharmacist before making changes; enlist their help in creating the most manageable plan.

Despite the benefits of most modern medications in maintaining health and managing chronic illness, no one wants their life to revolve around taking pills. Having a manageable schedule is a crucial step toward ensuring medications are taken as planned. In this way they will be the most helpful with the least impact on your parent's daily life.

(Remember, this list should be taken to every medical appointment.)

Step Three: *Pick a system to manage medications according to the schedule.*

To effectively manage medication so that your parent takes everything when and how it should be taken requires some organization. Whatever you set up as a system to manage medications, it has to be a system that works for your parent, even if you would prefer something else.

It is easy to forget to take medications. Six or more medications every day, for example, can make for a very complicated schedule. A system is essential.

There are some high tech solutions available that monitor or dispense pills with lights and sounds to tell the person when it is time to take a pill. You can also get smart phone apps that provide reminders when it is time for a pill. But you can also set up a simple system that works well. No one approach works for everyone. The important thing is to find a system that works for your parent.

You might do better with a pill box with compartments for morning, noon, dinner and bedtime. If the small slot is empty, then the pills were taken. But your parent might do better with one system for the morning and another for evening. This has to be her system. Unless you plan on becoming her constant reminder of when to take her medicine, you need a system that helps her remember to take the right pills when they are scheduled.

Your parent's system may be to keep morning pill bottles in the kitchen near her coffee pot, noon pill bottles on the kitchen table where she eats lunch, and evening pills on the side table by the chair where she usually sits in the evening. This may work but there are no checks and balances with this kind of system. Your parent will need to remember whether she took her pills each time they were due. However, if this system does work for her there is no reason to change it.

There are many options for pill boxes. You can find some at your local pharmacy and many more if you shop online. Most have compartments set up for anywhere from once a day to four times a day. Many people find these to be effective organizing tools.

If you decide to use one of the divided pillboxes, choose one with compartments large enough to hold all of the pills to be taken at one time. They come in different sizes. You don't want your parent to have to have two pillboxes if she takes quite a few different pills.

If your parent decides to use a pillbox it may be necessary to have an alternate system to use when he leaves the house. If he is active and away from home at a scheduled pill-taking time, this needs to be part of the plan. No one wants to carry their weekly medications around with them when they go to lunch or a senior center. There are one-day boxes that could be a good answer for times like this.

Some pharmacies will help. They may put medications into weekly pill boxes or put medications into a bubble pack dose system. A bubble pack system puts everything your parent takes at a particular time of day into one paper or plastic bubble.

Some of the bubble pack systems are easier to carry along when leaving the house. For example, they allow a person to tear off a single section with just the noon pills.

Bubble pack systems can be a problem, however, when medications change. If a pharmacy has put together a week's worth of dose packets and a dose changes or a medication is added or removed, the medications in the original bubble pack cannot be reused. The pharmacy will need to redo new dose packets. You might be able to work with your pharmacy to find a way to manage these changes. Just keep in mind this can be a problem.

Coordinating refills will also help your parent manage her medications. Coordinating refills means picking up multiple refills at the same time. Her pharmacist can help arrange this too. Just like she doesn't want to worry about taking medications every hour or two, she doesn't want to have the worry or burden of stopping by the pharmacist every week to ensure adequate supplies of all prescriptions are kept on hand.

Obtaining all medications from a single pharmacy and then asking for the pharmacist's help to put together the most manageable schedule could save a lot of time and headache.

Step Four: *Ask for a medication review at least annually.*

A review of every medication that your parent takes will help assure both you and your parent that he or she is taking the best mix of medications for her age and multiple medical conditions. Either your parent's doctor or pharmacist can conduct a complete review of her medications. It should include not only those medications prescribed by doctors but every non-prescription added to the list.

Starting with your pharmacist first can be helpful. Pharmacists know a lot about the medications people take and are very good at considering options for medications that can meet clinical needs and fit into a reasonable life routine.

To be sure the pharmacist has time for the review, and to discuss any potential questions that could arise, it is a good idea to arrange an appointment for this review at a time when the pharmacy is less busy.

At least once a year you should ask your parent's doctor to review her medications with the question, "Does she still need to take _____?" It is not unusual for the number of prescriptions to grow over time. It is wise to occasionally ask if a medication should still be taken. It might be one that your parent should discontinue.

It is not uncommon for people to needlessly continue to take a medication for years just because their physician never thought to tell them to stop taking it.

When a pharmacy calls for a renewal of a medication it typically gets renewed. Refills can even be automatic. Some pharmacies have a computerized trigger that prompts a refill even before the patient calls to request one. This is a convenience for those medications a person takes over a long time. But it can also lead to refills without anyone stopping to consider whether it is still in the person's best interest to keep taking it.

Again, using one pharmacy for all prescriptions helps. That way a pharmacist will see the listing of everything your parent takes when a new prescription is filled. If a medication could cause a potential interaction or problem, the pharmacist can contact your parent's doctor before filling the prescription. The pharmacist can even work with your parent's doctor to find a better solution.

A physician colleague of mine says that, if evaluated carefully, many elderly people could reduce the number of medications they take. The schedule for how they are taken can also be simplified. He believes that medications should help us lead a more functionally independent and satisfying life, not control our lives.

When older adults have reviews of the drugs they take, more than half of them benefit from simplifying the schedule for how they take their medications. Some of the ways the regimen can be simplified include changing dosage, changing the time of day a medication is taken, or changing the number of times per day a medication is taken.

If a medication needs to be taken at an odd time, like an hour before a meal, the pharmacist may be able to suggest an alternative medication to the physician. This can make it possible for your parent to take medications at fewer different times during the day.

While it is important for your parent to understand her medications, it is also important for family members to be familiar with them, especially if they take her to doctor's appointments. If you recall my own experience with my mother you know that there are times when family members can be asked to provide this information when a parent is unable or unwilling to give it.

Keep track of your parent's health in a personal health record

You will find it helpful to keep a record of health events, new diagnoses, changes in medications, and other information over time. You can find quite a few resources to create a personal health record if you search the internet.

A personal health record might begin as a simple document. But when you keep it over an extended period of time it will get larger and more complex. Even keeping a clean medication list can be a challenge. A medication stops and another starts so you cross out one and enter the new one. A few changes like this can result in a pretty messy looking list. Now add medical conditions, the questions asked at the last medical appointment and their answers. Plus all the notes from your parent's recent hospitalization. Soon you have a jumbled up, disorganized mess that is hard to use.

Avoid this by starting right. Thinking about the best sort of system that will work for you. Some people use an expandable folder with loose sheets of paper. This is a flexible approach that allows you to remove information you no longer need. But the risk, of course, is of dropping the folder and having everything fall out and become jumbled or lost.

Spiral notebooks work for some but they can quickly become impossible to organize. A notebook makes it hard to keep track of changes and events over time and gets hard to follow after multiple entries.

A three-ring binder can be made to work. It allows tabs and things can be moved around in it and you can insert new pages. But three-ring binders tend to eventually become too bulky for most people. If you choose a paper solution be sure to label it clearly. Include something like "If found, please contact _____." You want this to be easily identified for what it is. And if you take it to a medical appointment you want others to know it contains important information.

If you are tech savvy there are phone apps and computer programs for keeping track of personal health records. Whether or not they will work for you depends on how you prefer to keep track of things. Paper lists or computer files, which do you prefer? Are you a Rolodex or file cabinet kind of person? You know your preferences and how organized or disorganized you tend to be, so take your own strengths and weaknesses into account before you get started. Once you have decided on the system that will work best, it is time to put it in place.

The personal health record complements the *Go Folder* mentioned earlier (and will be explained in more detail in the next section). The personal health record adds the following:

Services. A listing of all of the services your parent receives from any health or community agency. Some examples include the van service she uses for medical appointments or personal travel, Meals on Wheels, grocery delivery service, and house cleaning service.

Records. Records of critical health information such as blood pressure measures, weight or other details your parent's doctor advises would be helpful to track. If you put these into a table you will be able to spot changes over time.

Notes. The largest section will be your notes. This includes notes about medical appointments, hospital care, and any information learned from your parent's doctors that you may want to reference. You can include the purpose of each medical appointment and the questions you developed with your parent in advance. After each visit you can record the information you learned during the appointment.

Not only will this record help you, it will help your parent and other family members. If you keep track of your parent's health experience you will have a good reference for her when questions arise. Also, family members who aren't as involved in the day-to-day support of your parent can get answers to questions they might have. You will also have a record of symptoms that can signal when appropriate medical follow-up is needed.

Create an all-in-one Go Folder

The best case scenario is that your parent will live a long life with only gradual decline, although this will likely require occasional interventions in a hospital setting. To reduce the stress during hospitalizations and to make sure important information accompanies your parent, it is wise to create a *Go Folder*.

A *Go Folder* can be a file folder, envelope, notebook or whatever makes sense to your parent. The folder should include the most important information pertinent to her care. You may choose to keep the *Go Folder* with her personal health record. This removes the need for duplication and possible omission in one place or the other.

Your parent's *Go Folder* should include the following eight categories of information:

1. Copies of health insurance cards and personal identification.

2. A list of your parent's medical diagnoses.

3. The medication list that was developed earlier. Again, this should include everything she takes

(including herbal supplements and over-the-counter medications).

4. A copy of your parent's healthcare power of attorney and any other advance directive documents she has completed.

5. Personal contact information including the names of family members and close friends. Anyone your parent wants to include as her close contacts. Be sure to make it clear whom to contact in an emergency.

6. Contact information for all of her physicians and their medical specialties.

7. Any other special instructions such as the need for eyeglasses or hearing aids, the use of assistive devices like walkers and canes, and known allergies.

8. The name and contact information for the person who will take care of your parent's pets and home if she is not there.

This *Go Folder* supports your parent in case she isn't able to speak for herself at the time of a medical crisis. This information should be clearly labeled and kept where it is easy to find when needed.

Whether you use a folder, large envelope or something else, what you use should be easy to see and identify as your parent's *Go Folder*. In large bold lettering label the folder "Vital Health Information for (your parent's name)(phone number)". Keep the *Go Folder* in an easy to see place, not in a drawer. Options that work well are the kitchen counter or a table by the front door. Once you pick a place, be religious about always keeping the *Go Folder* in that place.

To make sure it is easy to find, make a few labels. Blank name tags work well. Print in easy to read lettering something like "Vital Health Information folder located on kitchen counter" (or wherever you decide works best). Place a sticker on the front door, on the bathroom medicine cabinet, and on the refrigerator door. The stickers should be obvious so that emergency personnel entering your parent's home will see them and be able to quickly and easily find the *Go Folder*. Emergency personnel are trained to look for vital information, but they won't have time to search all over the house.

Keeping this information available for medical professionals to reference can help prevent error. It can also ensure your parent receives care according to her wishes. As an extra precaution it is a good idea for you as caregiver to have copies the materials in the Go Folder just in case it is forgotten when your parent is taken to the hospital.

Once you put these components together – medication management, personal health record and *Go Folder* – you will have the pillars of all-in caregiving to help you in your role as caregiver. You will be able to keep track of your parents' health and help them stay as healthy as possible. You will have helped your parents set up a system to support safe management of medications. You will have set up a way to keep track of her health and the changes in her health over time. And, you will have put together a *Go Folder* that can be taken along if she needs to go to a hospital. By working on these pieces hopefully you learned that none of them are difficult. And together they help you to be a stronger advocate and caregiver.

Becoming your parent's caregiver was not a role you planned for, or prepared to take on. You may not have taken on the role of caregiver completely voluntarily. You probably did not know that you would eventually assume responsibility for care decisions when you agreed to be your parent's healthcare agent. But becoming prepared you have learned to have confidence that the decisions you make along the way will be made according to the wishes of your parents. Knowing what is important to them makes the job of decision-making much less stressful for you.

You now know you can master the secrets of all-in caregiving through preparation. You know how to help your parent be a stronger partner in her own care. Your preparation will also help you protect your parents from the potential hazards of medical care in all the care settings where care is provided. And when you need to step up to make decisions for your parents you will do so with confidence. Because you know that your decisions for your parents's care are consistent with what they want for themselves.

By taking a constructive and positive approach to this role you can prepare for the uncertainties and unexpected things that are bound to happen. Better preparation will help you in every aspect of your caregiving role. It can also allow you to keep at least a semblance of balance in your own life.

Many people who have studied the role of the family caregiver will concur that your own stress will be reduced if you take time to exercise, enjoy nutritious meals, and maintain your own social connections.

Engage others to help you to help your parents when you can. Ask for help. Create a care network. You may be surprised who will respond. Family and friends will take responsibility for the many daily tasks that allow your parents to continue living their lives in the manner they choose.

If you struggle to find the time and motivation to take care of yourself as well as your family member who is in need there are people and agencies who can help. Most communities have multiple support groups for family caregivers. Participating in these groups allows you to share your concerns and hear from others how they manage situations similar to your own. Ask your local senior center, area agency on aging, hospital or religious organization about support groups in your community.

You can also turn to the internet for resources. The proven educational program *Powerful Tools for Caregivers* is available online[27] and may also be offered through classes in your community. You will find tips and advice through the Caregiver Action Network[28] as well as AARP.[29]

Success in your role as family caregiver includes an array of topics that may require additional reading. Understanding how to choose the best Medicare plan, care provider, or living setting goes beyond what could be provided here. That kind of information is readily available from other resources such as those mentioned above.

When you reflect on the time you spend as your parents' advocate and supporting them in their needs and desires, you may well find that this time of closeness and sharing is one of the most rewarding times in your relationship with them. Through shared responsibility, listening, and respect you will probably learn a lot about your parents that you never knew. You will come to see them less from the narrow lens of "your parents" and become more aware of them in the broader perspective of who they are and have been their whole lives.

Notes

[27] Powerful Tools for Caregivers (bit.ly/2y7HaRW). A proven education program for family caregivers offered in most states across the country. This educational program is designed to teach practical tools and strategies to help family caregivers develop plans and use tools to better handle the challenges of their caregiver role.

[28] Caregiver Action Network is a program of the Family Caregiver Alliance. (www.caregiver.org) The Network provides many tips and practical advice for families for everything from managing the change in your role to juggling work responsibilities.

[29] AARP (www.aarp.org) has education on topics ranging from policy changes to home safety to handling the emotional challenges to taking on the various new roles of caregiving.

Appendices

Appendices

A
7-point medication list

A medication list should be maintained for any person taking prescription medications as well as non-prescribed substances, such as vitamins, minerals or other food supplements. A properly maintained list of medications is an important aspect of keeping everything organized for both health and safety.

Entries made in pencil can be easily changed when necessary. This makes it more likely that the list will be properly maintained and kept up to date.

The person's name should appear prominently on the list and on any subsequent pages if the list extends to more than one page. Each person should have his or her own list. If there are two or more people in the same household who are under medical care, there should be a separate medication list for each person.

The following seven categories have been found helpful for a manageable medication list.

1. **Drug**. The name of the prescription or drug and the prescribed dosage. Keep the list up-to-date with the latest prescribed strength (i.e., "5 mg." or "one drop in each eye").

2. **Purpose**. "Why I take this drug."

3. **Date**. The date the drug first began to be taken or administered. If a dosage is changed, enter the date the new dosage began.

4. **Appearance**. What it looks like.

5. **Schedule**. When should the drug be taken or administered?

6. **Method**. Any conditions or circumstances related to the drug, such as "with food" or "with meals."

7. **Prescriber**. The name of the doctor who prescribed the medication.

Include prescription *and* non-prescription medicines such as over-the-counter medicines (vitamins, minerals and natural supplements like herbs).

The form that follows is an example of a hypothetical medication list format.

Appendix A. 7-point medication list

MEDICATION LIST for _____ NAME _____

Drug*	Purpose	Date	Appearance	Schedule	Method	Prescriber
Example: Lisinipril 5 mg	Blood pressure	2018	Small round white tablet	Before bedtime	with water	Dr Jones

*Include all prescription and over-the-counter medicines (vitamins, herbs, minerals, natural supplements, etc.).

B
Advance care planning in 4 easy steps

[Share this section with your parent or other loved one. This will help you both plan together for peace of mind and future guidance. The following will help your parent clarify her own thinking about her wishes for future care, to select the person she wants to speak for her, and the steps necessary to execute these wishes legally.]

You spent a lifetime caring for and about your family. You worked for them. You worried about them. You took care of them. Now there is one more thing you can do for them: *Let them know your wishes for how you would like to be cared for in the future.*

Most people alive today will live a long life. As you age you might become less able to take care of yourself. You will find, as we all do inevitably, that it becomes increasingly more difficult to make your healthcare decisions on your own. Make certain your loved ones know your wishes so they can honor them.

The most important thing you can do is plan ahead:

- So you can receive the care that is important to you and that matches your wishes.

- To help your family and friends understand your wishes to spare them from having to make tough choices when you can no longer make them yourself.

- To give you and your loved ones peace of mind.

It is not easy to talk about how you want to live at the last phase of life. But avoiding the conversation might actually make it harder in a time of a crisis. That's why the time to talk is now. Have a conversation now, before you experience a health crisis, before you are unable to share what is important to you. Doing this now will not only be best for you in the long run, it will also greatly reduce uncertainty and anxiety for those who care about you. They won't have to guess what you want because you will have provided them with direction. By planning ahead you can think about your choices to receive the care that you want.

Your advanced care plan – the 4 steps

Step 1. *Think about what is important to you and how you want to receive your care.*

Before you have a conversation with your loved ones, think about what is important in your life, as well as the kinds of healthcare that you want and don't want. Only you know what is important to you. The following questions can help you to think about, and then talk about your healthcare wishes. Consider each question and make notes to help you recall your thoughts when you talk with those close to you.

- What gives your life meaning and purpose? What helps you live well at this time in your life? What is it that you like to do and would like to be able to continuing doing?

Appendix B. Advance care planning in 4 easy steps

- What are your fears or worries? About the future as you become older and less able to care for yourself? About healthcare treatments?

- What about pain? If you are in a great deal of pain, would you prefer to be alert and tolerate the pain? Or would you rather have no pain even if that means taking pain killers that make you drowsy?

- Who are the people most important to you?

- Where do you want to live? Where would you prefer to live if you become unable to care for yourself? At home? In a nursing home, hospice, or someone else's home?

- Who or what sustains you? When you face serious decisions? To meet challenges in your life?

- How far do you want treatment to go? Would you always want every treatment possible to be provided for your care? Or are there circumstances when you would say "enough, no more"?

- Can you imagine a time when you would want your doctor to withhold or withdraw medical treatment? Even if that treatment would help you live a bit longer but in pain?

- Are there any situations when you would not want food or drink through a feeding tube or other artificial means?

As time goes by, you may have different answers to these questions. There are no right or wrong answers. After you think about these questions, your thoughts can be the basis for a conversation with the person who will speak for you, and with others who care about you, if you are unable to speak for yourself.

Step 2. *Select a person to speak for you if you are unable to speak for yourself.*

State law allows you to pick someone to act as your healthcare agent in the event you are unable to speak for yourself or make healthcare decisions. Your healthcare agent will be legally empowered to speak for you and make decisions about your healthcare. If you do not choose someone to speak for you as your agent, people who don't know you are likely to decide your care. Some decisions may be allowed by next of kin, but life sustaining care decisions might require intervention by courts of law who will make the decision.

Step 2a. Understand the responsibilities of your healthcare agent.

Your healthcare agent will have access to your medical information and records to make informed care decisions.

Your agent will have authority to make all healthcare decisions, unless you limit the agent's authority, or unless a court order overrides the decision.

Being a healthcare agent does not mean your agent is responsible to pay for your care or has any other responsibility for your personal business.

Your agent will make decisions to use or remove treatments that may extend your life, and whether you will have certain medical tests, treatments, or surgeries.

Step 2b: Choose someone you trust to be your healthcare agent.

Often people pick a friend or family member to be their agent. Keep in mind that not everyone makes a good agent. The following questions will help you choose your agent:

- Is the person someone you want by your side when you have important health decisions to make?

- Will this person follow your wishes, even if he or she doesn't agree with them?

- Will this person be strong enough to ask questions about your condition and about the choices that may affect your care?

- Will this person be able to speak up for you, to demand that your wishes are followed?

- Will this person be available when you need help with the decisions and challenges that you may face in the last years of your life?

- Does this person meet the age requirement in your state? The minimum age in most states is 18, but there is some variation. Check the law in your state for eligibility requirements.

Remember, this person cannot be your doctor or an employee of a healthcare provider responsible for your care, unless he or she is a family member.

Putting this person's name on your legal document does not ensure you have an agent who will represent your wishes. Have a conversation with the person you pick to be your agent. Share the role and responsibilities and make sure that he or she is willing to act for you. Keep in mind it is possible in many states to have two people serve in this role and you can also make it clear, if you wish, that the person you select is expected to consult with others.

Step 3. *Talk about your healthcare wishes.*

Only you should decide how you want to live the last years and months of your life. It is hard to have this discussion, but harder still for your family and friends to make decisions for you without knowing what you want.

Take a step toward peace of mind by beginning the conversation with your agent, your family and close friends. It may be awkward at first, so use this guide to help you with this conversation.

Ways to begin a conversation about your healthcare wishes:

"I'd like to talk with you about how I would like to be cared for if I become unable to speak for myself. Is that OK?"

"As I become older and face more health problems, I am concerned that you don't know what kind of care I would like. Could we talk about this now? It would make me feel better now, and might help you feel better later."

"Do you remember what happened to Aunt Mary when she was in the nursing home and couldn't feed herself? None of us knew what she would have wanted. I don't want you to have to go through that with me. That's why I want to talk about this now, while we can."

Your conversation with your agent does not have to be, and probably should not be, a one-time event. Your condition and healthcare needs will change over time and your opinions about your choices might also change. At least once a year discuss your wishes about what is important in your life and for your care. Talk about your choices for treatment or for comfort. Help your family and friends deal with tough choices by making your wishes known in advance.

The most important thing is to share your thoughts, concerns and wishes. Talking about it may be difficult. But the more you share, the more peace of mind you will have. And the more your caregivers will appreciate it later.

Step 4. *Put it in writing.*

Laws in every state are designed to make sure your wishes for care are respected. Through the use of what is known as a Durable Power of Attorney for Healthcare (also known as a Healthcare Proxy) you are permitted to name another person to make healthcare decisions, if you are no longer able to make decisions. These decisions apply to all healthcare treatments including services and procedures to diagnose or treat any physical or mental condition.

You can obtain your state's form through your doctor or through your state's Department of Health. Once you complete this form according to the instructions, the person you name will be eligible to serve as your healthcare agent. Your agent can make healthcare decisions for you only if your doctors decide you are not able to make healthcare decisions yourself.

You may include the name of a second person as the alternate agent. If you like, you may also add instructions for your healthcare agent to help make future healthcare decisions. If you wish to limit your agent's authority in any way, include instructions to that effect on the form. If you do not state any limitations, your agent will be allowed to make all healthcare decisions that you could have made, including the decision to consent to, or refuse, life-sustaining treatment.

It is especially important to discuss and write down your wishes about artificial nutrition (being fed through a tube) and artificial hydration (providing water through a tube). If this is not stated, your agent may not have the authority to make decisions about these treatments.

Talk to your doctor to make sure you understand your medical condition and treatments. You can make a very specific statement about your care wishes including specific instructions for different situations. Alternatively, you can simply state:

"I have discussed my wishes and preferences with my healthcare agent and alternate, and they know my wishes including those about artificial nutrition and hydration."

When the form is complete, you will need signatures of witnesses according to your state's requirements. Generally these witnesses are attesting to your signature with a statement that says you appear to have completed this form willingly. Neither your healthcare agent nor your alternate can sign as a witness. While lawyers will often offer completion of this form as part of the process of preparing a will, you do not need a lawyer or notary for your form to be legal.

What to do with your Durable Power of Attorney for Healthcare form:

- Make copies of this form for your agent and anyone else who may be involved with your care including your physician, members of your family, and your spiritual advisor.

- Provide a copy to your healthcare provider, hospital or clinic so it can be scanned into your medical record.

- Keep the original in a place that is easily found.

- Put a note in your wallet with your healthcare agent's name and the location of your form.

After your Durable Power of Attorney for healthcare form is signed and witnessed, you still have the right to make all your healthcare decisions as long as you are able to do so.

It is not easy to talk about how you want to live the last phase of life. But avoiding the conversation may actually make it harder for those you love.

The time to talk is now. Have a conversation before you experience a health crisis. Now you know and can share what is important to you. Later you might not be able to. Taking care of it now can greatly reduce the worries for those who care about you. And keep this in mind: If you don't share your wishes, how can they be respected?

Material in appendix B adapted from the Sharing Your Wishes educational materials. Used by permission. Original materials were developed by the author.

Index

advance care planning, 98, 102
Advance care planning in 4 easy steps, 104, 267
conversation, 102
Five Wishes®, 104
Go Wish™ game, 104
healthcare agent, 98, 123, 270
Next Step in Care™, 104
start conversations, 103, 272
The Conversation Project, 104
wishes may not be followed, 129
Advance care planning in 4 easy steps, 267
advance directive, 121
accessibility, 128, 274
artificial hydration and nutrition, 134, 221
do not resuscitate(DNR), 124
durable power of attorney for healthcare, 122, 273
healthcare proxy, 122
living will, 124
Physician Order for Life-Sustaining Treatment, 126
advance life planning conversation, 58
goals, 58
mulled familiarity, 58
preferences, 60
purpose, 63
questions, 60
aging in place, 13, 70
Americans with Disability Act standards, 73
home improvement, 72
home safety, 71
housing options, 70
moving, 69
risk, 78
support and services, 77
universal design, 73
aging-friendly neighborhoods, 74
Alzheimer's Association, 63
anger, 44
Ask Me 3, 175
Beers List, 165
care network, 47
family conflict 50/50 rule, 52
online resources, 51
Choosing Wisely - AGS, 166
chronic medical conditions, 83
cognitive decline ten early signs, 63
community resources, 27
daily living

activities, 25
instrumental
  activities, 25
dementia, 62
  ten early signs, 63
depression, 56
  withdrawal, 55
Do Not Resuscitate
  (DNR) form, 124
durable power of
  attorney for
  healthcare, 122
dwindles, 53

end-of-life care, 137
  hospice care, 141
  life's final
    moments, 147
  palliative care, 138
  where people die,
    144

falls, 33, 69, 76, 203
family caregiver, 1,
  16, 18, 256
  anger, 44
  conversation, 35,
    37
  fear, 43
  guilt, 45
  Powerful Tools for
    Caregivers, 258
  resentment, 46
family conflict 50/50
  rule, 52
fear, 43

Go Wish™ game, 104
grab bars, 73
guilt, 45

HIPAA, patient
  privacy, 133
home safety
  Americans with
    Disability Act
    standards, 73
  Home Safety
    Self-Assessment
    Tool, 73
hospital care, 185
  emergency care,
    188
  Go Folder, 190, 254
  hospitalist, 130
  keep notes, 192
  observation status,
    187
hospital care
  hazards, 192, 195
  bed rest, 198
  delirium and
    confusion, 204
  falls, 203
  incontinence and
    catheters, 209
  malnutrition and
    dehydration, 219
  medical mistakes,
    215
  medications, 213
  over-treatment, 86,
    224
  psychological
    impact, 222
  skin breakdown,
    207
hospital discharge
  and return home,
    229

food and beverage,
  237
instructions, 230
medications, 236
Next Step in Care
  text™, 239
hospitalist, 130

life choices, 56
life-sustaining
  treatments, 87, 106,
    109
  antibiotic therapy,
    119
  artificial hydration
    and nutrition, 112,
    134
  cardio-pulmonary
    resuscitation, 110
  kidney dialysis,
    117
  mechanical
    ventilators, 116
living will, 124
loneliness, 34

medical
  appointment, 169
  Ask Me 3, 175
  make notes, 179
  medications, 177
  prepare for a
    doctor's
    appointment, 170
  questions to ask
    the doctor, 172
  what to take, 173
medical care
  red flags, 156
medical care choices,
  83

Choosing Wisely, 166
Hard Choices for Loving People, 109
patient values, American Geriatrics Society, 92
pros and cons, 85, 89
treatment choice questions, 89
medical care decisions, 167
family consent laws, 122
self-care, 97
medication appointment
listen, 181
medication list form, 263
medications, 236
Beers List, 165
hazards, 213
medication list, 245
medication management, 241
medication review, 249
mental decline

dementia, 62
mental decline and dementia
ten early signs, 63
movement, increase difficulty moving, 75
simple movements, 75

Next Step in Care™, 136
nursing homes, 77

partner in care
become informed, 156, 161
person-centered care, 160
role of advocate, 163
take responsibility, 157
physician medical practice, 151
care guidelines, American Geriatrics Society, 165
electronic medical records, 152
improving care for older adults, 165

medical homes, 154
Physician Order for Life-Sustaining Treatment (POLST), 126
pillars of all-in caregiving
Go Folder, 190, 254
medication management, 236, 241
medication list, 245, 263
medication review, 249
organized system, 247
personal health record, 251
power of attorney, 101
Powerful Tools for Caregivers, 258

resentment, 46
risk, 78
role reversal, 20

Share the Care™, 49
slow medicine, 90

Made in the USA
Las Vegas, NV
19 December 2023